S.S. GREWAL (born 17 August 1947) is a former IAS officer who quit the bureaucracy to devote himself full-tilt to the stock market. He has an educational background spanning science, engineering, literature and economics, and has been a practicing investment consultant since 1985. He lives in Chandigarh and devotes all his time to managing his stock market investments.

Mr. Grewal is also the author of three bestselling books on the stock market, including *Making Money on the Stock Market: A Practical Handbook* (1983), *Successful Stock Market Investing* (1987) and *The Thinking Investor* (1995), all published by Vision Books. He wrote a widely-read column on the stock markets in *The Tribune* for over three years.

NAVJOT GREWAL (born 17 September 1951) is a specialist in industrial psychology and has been a keen stock market investor. Along with her husband S. S. Grewal, she co-authored *Successful Stock Market Investing.* She now assists her husband in researching for his books and other investing work.

Profitable Investment in Shares

A Beginner's Guide

S. S. Grewal
Navjot Grewal

www.visionbooksindia.com

www.vision**books**india.com

Disclaimer

All investments are subject to risk. The author and the publisher disclaim all legal or other responsibilities for any losses which readers may suffer by investing in any portfolio and / or tax planning schemes suggested in this book. Readers are, therefore, advised to seek professional guidance before making any specific investments.

First Published 1984
2nd Revised Edition 1986
3rd Revised Edition 1989
4th Revised Edition 1990
5th Revised Edition 1994
6th Revised Edition, 2004
Reprinted 2005 (thrice), 2006 (thrice),
2007 (thrice), 2008 (twice), 2009, 2010, 2011, 2013, 2015, 2020, 2024, 2025
2026

ISBN 10: 81-7094-573-9
ISBN 13: 978-81-7094-573-4

Published by
Vision Books Pvt. Ltd.
(Incorporating Orient Paperbacks and CARING imprints)
24 Feroze Gandhi Road, Lajpat Nagar 3
New Delhi 110024, India.
Phone: (+91-11) 2984 0821 / 22
e-mail: visionbooks@gmail.com

Printed and bound at TACT Printers, Noida

Contents

Author's note on the sixth edition

This book was originally written in 1984 and revised and updated five times earlier. These revisions were necessitated by the sea change that has taken place in the investment scene in India in the last two decades. The stock market booms of 1985-86, 1990, 1992 and 2000 which cumulatively multiplied the average wealth of shareholders more than 40 times in the last 24 years and expanded the Indian shareholder population from 2 million to 50 million, also considerably altered the parameters, perceptions and yardsticks on which this book had earlier been based. This sixth new edition of the book now fully reflects the changed investment environment and should be of even more practical use to the reader. All the book's chapters have been thoroughly revised and updated. New chapters on investing in mutual funds, investor grievances and remedies, and tips for successful investing have been added along with an expanded Appendix giving more data for the investor.

Even though investment conditions, attitudes and opportunities often change over time and vary greatly from place to place, fundamental investment principles and basic "rules of the game" nearly always remain the same. In that sense, the main core of this book will always remain unchanged and should continue to be an evergreen and perennial guide for helping beginners find their way through the complexities and pitfalls of the stock market jungle.

Chandigarh — S. S. Grewal
May 2004 — Navjot Grewal

Preface

Are you one of those who wants to invest in shares but doesn't know quite how to go about it? If so, then this book is meant for you. That is why we have called it Profitable Investment in Shares: A Beginner's Guide. It presumes no previous knowledge of the subject on your part. We have tried to explain what investment in stock markets is all about in simple, clear and concise language and have avoided, as far as possible, the use of mathematics and technical jargon.

You don't need to be an economist, a chartered accountant, or a mathematical wizard to profit from shares. In fact, most people who have made great fortunes in the stock markets had no specialised knowledge in any of these fields. If they could make money, so can you! All it requires is common sense, and a willingness to spend some time and effort in collecting and analysing information on companies and their business environment. The book shows you how to go about it.

While writing this book, we have made use of information and materials from *Making Money on the Stock Market* by S.S. Grewal, one of the co-authors of this book. We have also, at places, made use of information contained in the web sites of the Bombay Stock Exchange, National Stock Exchange and SEBI, and in *The Economic Times*, *The Business Standard* and *Financial Express*. We gratefully acknowledge our debt to these publications.

This book is dedicated to our parents, and our two children, Priya and Ishwar.

Patiala — S.S. GREWAL

3 March 1984 — NAVJOT GREWAL

INTRODUCTION

Answering some basic questions

Let us begin with some basic questions you are likely to ask.

What are shares?

In everyday language, when we talk of shares we normally refer to equity shares or ordinary shares of a company. The terms shares and stocks essentially mean the same thing, the latter being a more common American usage.

An equity share is evidence of ownership in a company. The physical evidence of this ownership is a document called the share certificate. Nowadays, shares are usually kept in electronic, or dematerialised, form with a depository participant (banks, brokers, financial institutions) of the National Securities Depository Limited (NSDL). However, if one wants one can still hold shares in the physical form which has your name endorsed on it, and is proof that you are a part-owner of the company. Your ownership rights are proportionate to the number of shares you own. Suppose you purchase 100 shares in a company called XYZ Ltd, which has issued 10,000 shares, then you would own 1 per cent of the company. In short, it would mean that you own 1 per cent of its land, factory, equipment, patents, bank balances and all its other assets. Therefore when you invest in shares, you are actually purchasing a fractional ownership of the company.

Companies issue shares of a certain fixed denomination, called face value or par value of that share, which is clearly indicated on a share certificate in the physical form. Most shares of Indian companies have a face value of Rs. 10. Recently, however, some companies have split their Rs. 10 shares into shares of Rs. 5, Rs. 2 and even Re. 1. Face value or par value is the nominal value of the share in the books of the company. It is important to understand that it bears no relationship to the share's market price which fluctuates all the time. Dividends, however, are issued on the par value of the share and not its market value. It continues to retain this value, so far as the company is concerned, a share continues to be accounted for in its books at its face value irrespective of the price at which it may later be bought or sold in the stock markets.

It is important to understand that par value bears no relationship to the share's market price which fluctuates all the time.

What is investment?

Investment essentially refers to what you do with your savings in order to preserve them and make them grow or yield an income. If you keep your savings in the form of cash, they are certainly going to diminish in value because the purchasing power of money is constantly going down as a result of inflation. (The value of money is judged by the quantity of goods and services you can buy with it). Therefore if you want to maintain or increase the value of your savings, you have to keep them in forms other than cash. This is what investment is all about, deployment of your savings with the intention of preserving or increasing their value. This deployment can be done by using your savings to buy land, residential property, commercial property, gold, jewellery, works of art, fixed deposits in banks and companies, shares, bonds, in fact, anything whose value is likely to either remain constant or appreciate with time.

Investment also refers to using one's savings with the intention of earning an income. For example, if you use your savings to buy a house, it will not only appreciate in value, but it can also give you a monthly income in the form of rent. Similarly, investments in bank deposits, company deposits, debentures and shares will also give you regular income. On the other hand, investments in gold, jewellery or works of art appreciate in value but do not provide any income.

Accordingly, as an investor you have to decide whether you want your investment to appreciate in value, to give you a regular income, or a combination of both. To decide this you will have to make an assessment of what your future requirements for money are going to be like. It is only then that you will know to what extent you want your savings to appreciate in value, and to what extent you want these to provide a regular income. Having done so, you then have to decide on how and where to deploy your savings so that your future requirements for money can be best met. This, in essence, is what the art of investment is all about.

Why has investment become so important now?

There was a time, in the 1930s, when prices remained more or less constant. They did rise marginally but the rise was too small to have a significant impact on the cost of daily living. As a result most people felt economically secure and did not feel the necessity to take investment seriously. In the 1960s, this scenario underwent a drastic change. Prices began rising steadily and continuously, and the value of the rupee dropped sharply. The economic security of the fixed-income groups disappeared. The 1970s and the early 1980s saw a further acceleration in these trends. Consumer prices have risen by over ten times in the last 33 years. In terms of purchasing power, the worth of a rupee had fallen to only around 4 paise in 2004 as compared to 1960. In the forty years from 1960 to 2000, the annually compounded rate of inflation has been around 7-8 per cent.

It is now quite clear to most people that inflation has come to stay, and to stay permanently though after forty years of high inflation there is a possibility of a lower rate of inflation in the 2000s. Salaries and pensions are no longer adequate for meeting daily needs as they once were. Hard work, thrift and accumulated savings are no longer enough to provide for one's future. Savings have to be intelligently invested and you have to actively manage your investments if you are to succeed in increasing, or at least in preserving, the purchasing power of your savings. You have not only to make sure that the rupee value of your savings grows with time, but also that the rate of their growth is higher than the rate of inflation. If the rate of inflation is 8 per cent, your after-tax income must increase by at least 10 per cent to 12 per cent if you want to improve your standard of living.

This is the main reason why it has become essential for everyone to acquire a basic knowledge of investing. You will find it much easier to cope with the economic problems of the future if you know where and when to invest, and also how to manage your investments efficiently. In this book, we focus on profitable investment in shares.

CHAPTER 1

The case for investing in shares

Your capital grows quickly

Returns from investments in shares come in two forms — capital appreciation and dividends. Capital appreciation takes place when there is an increase in the price of your shares. For example, if you buy 100 shares of XYZ Ltd. for Rs. 1,000 and later sell them for Rs. 1,800, there is a capital appreciation of Rs. 800 or 80 per cent. This is also referred to as capital gains or capital appreciation.

When you invest in shares, your capital grows quickly — much faster than in most other forms of investment. Sometimes the growth can be spectacular, going even as high as 1,000 per cent per annum. People are attracted to shares precisely because they offer exciting possibilities of getting rich.

How much money can you expect to make from your investment in shares?

To answer this question, let us look at the performance of five well-known companies in the eight-year period from 1 January 1996 to 31 December 2003 (*See* Table1.1). This period is long enough to cover every kind of economic mishap, and a number of booms and depressions. If you had bought shares worth Rs. 1,000 in each of these companies at their prevailing prices on 1 January 1996, the value of your investment of Rs. 5,000 would have multiplied by 23 times and grown to Rs. 1,15,308 on 31 December 2003 giving you a capital appreciation of 2,206 per

Table 1.1

Company		*Amount Invested* on 31 Jan. 1996 *(In Rs.)*	*Value as on* 31 December *2003 (In Rs.)*	*Appreciation*
Dr. Reddy's Lab	:	Rs. 1,000	Rs. 13,352	+ 1,235 %
Wipro	:	Rs. 1,000	Rs. 14,382	+ 1,338 %
Infosys Technologies	:	Rs. 1,000	Rs. 76,235	+ 7,523 %
ITC	:	Rs. 1,000	Rs. 5,069	+ 407 %
Reliance Industries	:	Rs. 1,000	Rs. 6,270	+ 527 %
		Rs. 5,000	Rs. 1,15,308	+ 2,206 %

cent. In other words, your capital would have grown at a compound rate of 48 per cent per annum. In addition, you would have also earned a substantial amount through dividends during this period.

Let us now turn to a comprehensive view of the returns from shares. In the last 26 years, the BSE Sensitive Index (Sensex) has appreciated by approximately 60 times giving an annualised compounded return of around 17 per cent. This kind of return is achievable by the average investor and outclasses the return that he can possibly hope to earn from real estate, gold, collectibles, bonds, etc. Table 2 gives an idea of what an average investor could have earned, and probably did earn, during the last seventeen years. The figures in Table 1.2 are based on the capital appreciation recorded by the BSE Sensitive Share Price Index.

We have found through experience that a reasonably intelligent and well-informed stock market investor can, on an average, double his money in four to five years, or so. There are many who do even better. It all depends on how much knowledge and experience you have, and the time and effort you are prepared to spend on managing your investments.

Investments in shares enable you to keep well ahead of inflation. This is because share prices normally rise with inflation. By

Table 1.2

Calendar Year	*Capital Appreciation*	*Calendar Year*	*Capital Appreciation*
1987	- 18 %	1996	-1 %
1988	+ 51 %	1997	+ 19 %
1989	+ 17 %	1998	- 17 %
1990	+ 35 %	1999	+ 64 %
1991	+ 84 %	2000	- 21 %
1992	+ 37 %	2001	- 18 %
1993	+ 32 %	2002	+ 4 %
1994	+ 14 %	2003	+76%
1995	- 21 %		

Note: 1. Above data is as per monthly closing prices

2. Rs. 1,000 invested on 1 January 1987 would have grown to Rs. 12,567 by 31 December, 2003 giving a compound rate of growth of around 16 per cent per annum.

investing in shares you can ensure that the value of your savings does not get eroded over time by inflation. This is a big advantage that shares have over other traditional forms of investment, such as bank deposits, post office savings schemes, etc.

You get income too

Investments in shares not only give capital appreciation; it also gives income in the form of dividends. Dividend is the amount that a company distributes every year to its shareholders out of the profits it earns. It is usually expressed as a percentage of the face value of the share, or in rupees per share. To get a clear idea of what dividend means, let us assume that you own 100 equity shares of face value of Rs. 10 each in XYZ Ltd. Now if the company declares a dividend of 20 per cent or Rs. 2 per share, you will get a dividend of Rs. 200.

It is not necessary for a company to declare a dividend every year. Companies which make losses usually skip the payment of dividends. However, most profit-earning companies usually give an annual dividend to their shareholders. Some companies even split this annual dividend into two instalments, called interim dividend and final dividend. Most Indian companies usually give dividends ranging from 10 per cent to 30 per cent. It all depends upon the amount of profits the company earns, and the policy adopted by its management on how much of these profits it can afford to distribute to its shareholders.

As a rule-of-thumb, the amount you are likely to get as dividends every year will normally be around 1 to 2 per cent of the market value of your shares. For example, if you have shares in various companies whose current market value is Rs. 50,000 then you can expect around Rs. 500 to Rs. 1,000 as the total dividend from these companies. This is a useful rule to remember. It comes in handy when you want to make a quick mental calculation on how much income you are likely to get by way of dividends on your stock market investments.

Investing in shares is not speculation

There is a common tendency to look upon the buying and selling of shares as speculation. Some people even goes to the extent of calling it gambling. This is simply not true.

When you buy a share after making a proper assessment of a company's future prospects, your risk is minimal and limited. When you do so on the basis of insufficient knowledge, incomplete analysis, a "hunch" or a "feeling", the risks are naturally much greater. The former is investment, the latter speculation. Gambling is only an extreme form of speculation. The difference between investment and speculation really lies in the degree of risk that you are willing to accept for attaining your goal. The investor takes calculated risks and plays safe in return for moderate profits. The speculator deliberately takes high risks in the expectation of getting disproportionately greater profits. In the stock markets, the speculator generally tries to make short-term profits out of price fluctuations and usually ignores dividends. In addition, he often plays around with borrowed money instead of using his own funds. On the other hand, an investor generally uses his own money, and buys shares with the intention of earning both long-term capital gains and dividends. These are the essential differences between investment and speculation.

In the stock markets, both investors and speculators are operating all the time. However, it is not necessary that you should speculate. In fact, we strongly advise you against it. If you buy and sell shares on the basis of sufficient knowledge and analysis, your risks remain under control and your expected gains more predictable. In fact, in the stock market, long-term investors very rarely lose any money at all, whereas speculators more often than not do. This book is written for investors. Its objective is to provide a new investor with the essential knowledge and techniques required for making a proper analysis before investing, so that risks are reduced and gains made more certain.

It is a liquid investment

A liquid investment is one which can easily be sold. If an investment cannot be readily converted into cash it is often worthless. Liquid investments also have other advantages. They give you a feeling of security because they enable you to change your mind and correct your mistakes — in short, they give you flexibility for coping with the ever-changing economic conditions.

Shares are one of the most liquid forms of investment. They are much easier to buy and sell than real estate or works of art. Investments in social security certificates, debentures, national savings certificates, fixed deposits in banks and companies are basically illiquid in nature, because they are made for a fixed period of time and cannot be readily converted into cash before the expiry of such period.

However, all shares are not equally liquid; some are more liquid than others. Real liquidity is only found amongst what are called "active" shares. Active shares are those in which transactions take place frequently on the various stock exchanges. These are about 1,500 or so in number, and constitute the most liquid forms of investment available in India today. If you confine your investments to these shares, as you should, you can ensure liquidity of your investment.

You can ensure the safety of your capital

Are share investments safe? Do they provide adequate protection against the risk of a capital loss? They do, if you follow the three basic principles:

- Liquidity,
- Long-term investment strategy, and
- Diversification of your portfolio.

Liquidity ensures safety of capital because it enables you to convert your investment into cash at the slightest fear or hint of a capital loss.

A long-term investment strategy protects your portfolio from the temporary fluctuations and vagaries of the market.

Diversification reduces the risk of a capital loss, by spreading your investment over a large number of companies run by different business houses, operating in different fields — like chemicals, shipping, engineering, steel, paper, etc. — and with plants located in different geographical regions of the country. The wisdom behind diversification of investments is the same as that expressed in the oft-repeated aphorism "Never put all your eggs in one basket." By diversifying your investments you will usually find that even if you incur unexpected capital losses in one or two companies, these are likely to be more than adequately made up by gains in others.

It is easy to manage

Investments in shares are easier to manage and control than other forms of investment. Shares, being movable property, are easier to carry from place to place. Also, in case of loss, theft, or damage, you can easily obtain duplicate share certificates from the concerned companies. You don't need to keep share certificates in safes and bank lockers, or insure them like gold and jewellery. In the case of listed shares, investors in any case find it convenient to dematerialise their shares and keep them with a depository participant (bank, financial institution or broker). It is as easy and safe to keep shares in this form as keeping money in a bank. Managing share investments is much easier and less complicated than the management of property and real estate. You don't have to worry about problems, like property taxes, upkeep of buildings, and eviction of unwanted tenants.

However, there are a few things you will be required to do for managing your share investments efficiently. Apart from looking after your demat holdings and keeping track of dividends, you have to keep yourself reasonably well-informed not only on the performance and working of the companies in which you own shares, but about other prominent companies also. This will ensure that your buying and selling of shares is done at the right time and at the right prices. A list of newspapers, magazines, and other sources of investment information is given in Appendix A. You can also subscribe to investment newsletters and other investment advisory and counselling services to help you take correct and timely investment decisions.

You don't need a lot of money to start

The stock markets hold out attractive opportunities for the small investor because share investments do not necessarily require large sums of money. Investments in shares and the building of a portfolio can even be made with amounts as small as Rs. 100. In fact, most of the 50 million or so Indian shareholders are small investors with investments ranging from Rs. 10,000 to Rs. 50,000. Shares can now be bought even one at a time since the stock exchange authorities have now done away with the earlier concept of market lots and odd lots. This is a big advantage that investment in shares has over investment in property and real estate. The latter forms of investment require large sums of money and have now clearly moved beyond the reach of most middle-class investors. Stock markets are also better organised and their working is more closely regulated by the government and Securities and Exchange Board of India (SEBI) than those of property or commodity markets. Even the activities of stockbrokers come under a closer watch than those of property agents, etc.

Again, investments in shares are ideally suited to the requirements of genuine middle-class investors, as these don't involve transactions in "black" or unaccounted money. This is not always possible while buying and selling property and real estate.

Finally, investments in shares usually provide investors certain exclusive tax advantages which other forms of investments don't. The stock market investor, particularly the long-term equity investor, operates virtually in a tax haven. The specific tax advantages vary from time to time and you can check the latest status at any of the investment websites listed in Appendix A.

CHAPTER 2

Important things every investor should know

What is a company?

A company is a form of business organisation. It is basically an association of individuals called shareholders who get together for the purpose of running a particular business. A company is managed by a board of directors, which consists mostly of elected representatives of the shareholders.

The money that a company raises for starting and running its business is called capital. This is initially raised from the shareholders who jointly own the company. The amount so raised is called the equity capital of the company. Companies also raise capital by borrowing from the public, banks and other financial institutions. They raise money from the public either through fixed deposits or by selling debentures. The people who buy debentures are called debenture holders. Debenture holders are creditors of the company because the company owes them money — whereas shareholders are owners of the company.

Liabilities and rights of shareholders

A company has an independent legal existence of its own, quite distinct from that of its shareholders. This means that a company can, without in anyway involving its shareholders, enter into contracts, buy, sell and own property, engage in litigation, or incur debts. A shareholder cannot be held personally responsible or liable for the actions of a company, or any of its directors or employees. The liability of the shareholder to his company is limited to the value of the share he holds in the company. This is a purely financial liability which is fully discharged when the shares are bought — it ceases to exist after that. This means that if you buy 100 shares of face value Rs. 10 each in XYZ Ltd., then your financial liability to the company is Rs. 1,000 which is fully discharged by you on the purchase of these shares. Thereafter, if XYZ Ltd. becomes bankrupt and goes into liquidation, the worst that can possibly happen to you is that the price of your shares may fall to zero and you may not be able to recover your initial investment of Rs.1,000. Under no circumstances can you be asked to pay any additional money to XYZ Ltd. or to its creditors. This is the essence of the concept of "limited liability". All companies are required by law to use the word "Limited" (or its common abbreviation "Ltd.") after their names to show that the financial liability of its shareholders is limited. So when you buy shares in a company, you can do so with full confidence that you will not be incurring unlimited or unforeseen financial liabilities, or getting involved with the company's financial and legal problems in any other way.

As a shareholder you can transfer your ownership rights by selling your shares to others. Shares are movable property which can be bought, sold, gifted, bequeathed or transferred in any other manner permitted by law. Since the company has an independent existence of its own, it is not affected by any changes in its owners. Initially when a company is formed, shares in the company can be bought at their face value by making payments directly to the company. This is how companies raise their initial financial capital. Thereafter, the company is not affected by any subsequent transactions in which its shares are bought and sold in the stock exchanges. For example, if a Rs. 10 share of a company is sold in the stock market at Rs 3,000 each, it does not mean that the company is now 300 times richer. All it means is that buyers of its shares consider that the company has a bright future and its shares are worth the high price they are paying for it.

Public limited and private limited companies

There are two types of companies, public limited and private limited. It is mandatory for a private limited company to end its name with the words "private limited", while a public limited company simply ends its name with the word "limited".

When we talk of investment in shares, we are actually referring to investment in shares of public limited companies. The shares of private limited companies are neither quoted on the stock exchange, nor are they freely available for sale. In fact, private limited companies are expressly prohibited from selling their shares to the public. On the other hand, shares of public limited companies are widely held by the public and are normally freely available for sale and purchase on the stock exchange.

Register of members

Shareholders are often also referred to as members of the company. Every company is required to maintain a register of members where the names, addresses and other relevant particulars of its shareholders and their shareholdings are recorded. Nowadays this information is also maintained by the two depositories: the NSDL (National Securities Depository Ltd.) and the CSDL (Central Securities Depository Ltd.). This makes it easier for the depositories to service the shareholders with respect to dividends, rights and bonus shares. In fact, most listed companies have now transferred their shares to the depositories who, in turn, keep a record of the shareholders and their particulars.

Annual report

Every company prepares an annual report on its functioning and accounts and sends it to each of its shareholders well before the date fixed for the company's annual general body meeting.

The annual report comprises the:

- Directors' Report,
- Auditors' Report, and
- A Fully-audited Balance Sheet and Profit and Loss Account of the company for the previous year.

The annual report is one of the most important and useful documents for a shareholder and a prospective investor.

The directors' report gives information on the general condition of the company's business, its future prospects, proposals regarding declaration of dividends, allocation to reserves and other information having a bearing on the finances and operations of the company.

The auditors' report informs the shareholders whether the accounts of the company give a "true and fair" view of the state of the company's finances at the close of the company's accounting year, and of the profits made by the company during the year.

Preference shares and equity shares

There are two categories of shares:

1. Preference shares, and
2. Equity shares.

Preference shares give a fixed rate of dividend, which is currently around 6 to 8 per cent per annum. Preferential shares give a right to their holders to receive dividends and repayment of capital in case the company is wound up in preference to equity shareholders. Companies which make losses are sometimes not in a position to pay any dividends to their preference shareholders. To provide for such an eventuality, companies issue what are called cumulative preference shares. Unpaid dividends on these shares do not lapse, but are allowed to accumulate till the company is in a position to clear all the arrears of accumulated dividends. A company cannot pay any dividends to its equity shareholders until all such arrears of accumulated preference dividends have been paid. This gives added security to preference shareholders by assuring them of their fixed dividend, irrespective of the extent of losses which the company may incur.

The share capital of a company is not refunded to the shareholder so long as the company is in existence. However, an exception is usually made in the case of holders of redeemable preference shares as their share capital can be refunded, or "redeemed" from the company after a certain fixed period of time.

Equity shares, on the other hand, don't carry a fixed rate of dividend. In fact, equity shareholders cannot claim dividends as a matter of right. Since equity shareholders are the owners of the company, they are entitled to all the residual profits and accumulated reserves of the company after all its obligations to its creditors and preference shareholders have been met.

Equity shareholders form a bulk of the shareholders of a company. They exercise full voting power on all important matters affecting the company. When a company makes large profits, the lion's share goes to its equity shareholders. Conversely, when profits go down it is the equity shareholders who have to bear the brunt and are often deprived of even a modest dividend.

In growing and expanding companies, an equity shareholder gets a much higher rate of return on his investment than does a preference shareholder. The latter gets only his fixed rate of dividend, whereas the former gets the double benefit of substantial capital appreciation, plus higher dividends. His shareholding also expands with the addition of rights and bonus shares. A preference shareholder does not get the benefits of capital appreciation on his investment. Thus an equity shareholder bears higher risks than the preference shareholder and, in return, is rewarded with higher profits. Finally, it is the equity shareholder who experiences the excitement and thrills of stock market investment.

Rights shares

Companies often require additional funds for their working capital, or for their expansion and diversification programmes. They sometimes raise these funds by the sale of additional equity shares on a "rights basis" to its shareholders. Such shares are called "rights shares" because the company's shareholders have a prior right to buy these shares by virtue of their existing shareholding. The number of rights shares offered to each shareholder is directly proportionate to the number of equity shares he owns. Rights shares could either be offered at par, or at a premium. When such shares are offered for sale at their face value, they are said to be offered at par, and when the sale price is higher, they are said to be offered at a premium. Premium is the difference between the issue price of a share and its face value. In order to make the issue attractive, the price of rights shares is invariably fixed at a level below the prevailing market price of the company's share. The issue of rights shares increases the equity capital of the company but does not dilute an existing shareholder's proportionate ownership in the company, if he subscribes to his rights entitlement in full.

Bonus shares

Companies do not generally distribute their entire profits to the shareholders as dividends. A fairly large part of the profit is retained and added on to what is commonly called the reserves of the company. As the name indicates, reserves are back-up funds which a company keeps for meeting unforeseen increases in expenditure, and for financing its future expansion or diversification programmes. Over the years, most profit-making companies build up large reserves. There is also a sizeable increase in their assets, sales and volume of business. When such growth takes place, companies often find that their equity capital is too small compared to the expanded size of their business operations. It is not advantageous for companies to operate a continuously expanding business on a narrow capital base. Therefore, in order to expand their equity capital they capitalise a part of their reserves by issuing bonus shares to their shareholders. Bonus shares, as the name suggests, are issued free to existing shareholders in proportion to the number of shares held by them. It is essentially a book transfer by which a sum of money equal to the value of the bonus shares is transferred from the reserves to the equity capital in the company's books of accounts. The issue of bonus shares enlarges a shareholder's shareholding without any dilution in his proportionate ownership of the company.

The issue of bonus shares almost always leads to a fall in the market price of a share. This does not, however, adversely affect the shareholder because such a fall in the market price is more than offset by the increase in the size of his shareholding.

To illustrate how this happens, let us assume that you own 100 shares in XYZ Ltd. when it issues bonus shares in the ratio of 1:1. Let us also assume the market price to be Rs. 50 per share prior to the bonus issue. With the issue of bonus shares, your shareholding doubles to 200 shares. At the same time, the market price of the shares would probably fall to Rs. 25 per share. Even though the price has fallen, you do not lose because the value of your shareholding remains at Rs. 5,000. The fall in price from Rs. 50 to Rs. 25 per share is fully compensated by the increase in your shareholding from 100 to 200 shares. Actually, share prices generally do not fall in the same proportion in which bonus shares are issued. In this case, the ex-bonus price of XYZ shares would probably fall to around Rs. 27 per share.

Companies usually continue to pay the same rate of dividend after the issue of bonus shares as they were paying prior to the issue. This benefits the shareholder because he gets the same rate of dividend on a larger shareholding. A company will not normally issue bonus shares unless it is confident that its future growth prospects justify an expansion in its equity capital. Therefore, the expectation of a bonus issue by any company normally creates a climate of optimism and cheer in the stock markets and usually results in a rise in the price of a company's shares just before or upon the announcement by it of a bonus issue.

The stock exchange

The stock exchange is basically a marketplace for shares and securities. That is why it is also called a stock market. Just like any other market, it brings together the potential buyers and sellers of securities. The term "security" is a broad, generic term covering equity shares, preference shares, debentures and bonds issued by government, semi-government and local authorities. For all practical purposes now there are only two nation-wide stock exchanges in India: the Bombay Stock Exchange (BSE) and the National Stock Exchange (NSE).

Unlike other markets, however, you are not permitted to buy or sell shares directly in a stock exchange. According to the stock exchange rules you have to do so through a licensed member of the stock exchange called a stockbroker; or through his registered sub-broker. The stockbroker is authorised to buy and sell shares on behalf of others on a commission basis. This commission, or fee, is called brokerage. The brokerage rates are fixed by the stock exchanges. The maximum brokerage allowed by the stock exchanges can be verified from their web sites. At the time of writing, the maximum brokerage permitted was 2.5 per cent of the transaction value.

Trading in recognised stock exchanges in India is confined only to listed securities. Companies have to list their securities with one or more stock exchanges in order to make them eligible for trading. Listing is not a statutory obligation for public limited companies but most of them prefer to get their securities listed because of the numerous advantages and benefits of doing so. Listing not only gives easy marketability and liquidity to a share, but trading in it is subject to the regulation and control of the stock exchanges authorities. As such, listed securities enjoy greater confidence among investors.

Reading daily market quotations

The prices at which shares are transacted on the stock markets get wide coverage in daily newspapers. Financial newspapers, like *The Economic Times*, *Business Standard*, *The Financial Express*, and *The Hindu Business Line*, of course, give a more comprehensive and detailed coverage. Stock market quotations in a financial newspaper will typically give you the following information:

1. Name of the company;
2. Separate set of quotations for BSE and NSE;
3. BSE code number assigned to the company;
4. Closing price of the previous day;
5. Opening price of the previous day;
6. High and low prices of the previous day;
7. Value of shares traded;
8. Number of trades that took place in the share;
9. Volume of shares traded;
10. Current P/E ratio; and
11. High/low prices of the year, or the past 52-weeks.

It is quite easy to read these quotations since almost all these newspapers provide easy-to-understand explanatory notes.

Multinational companies (MNCs)

As an investor you would frequently come across the term MNC in newspapers and magazines. MNC is an abbreviation which stands for multinational companies which were earlier also known as FERA companies when the erstwhile Foreign Exchange Regulation Act (FERA) was in force. FERA put a number of restrictions on the operations of companies owned and controlled by foreigners. An MNC is a company in which foreigners held more than 40 per cent of its equity capital. Now, however, such restrictions on foreign holdings in Indian companies have been removed. Many MNCs have foreign holdings going up to 80 per cent.

Most Indian subsidiaries of multinational corporations are now called MNCs, and their shares remain, by and large, good investments.

Blue chips

This is another frequently used term though there is no standard definition of what a blue chip is. It is a term that is loosely used for companies that are sound investments in every respect. Companies that are large in size, technologically advanced, have professional management of a high calibre, and have built up a reputation for growth, regular payment of high dividends, and integrity in business dealings would normally qualify to be labelled as blue chips. However, no two investors would ever agree on where to draw the line separating blue chip companies from the others. It all finally boils down to subjective and personal preferences.

Bulls and bears

Most stock exchange speculators can be broadly grouped into two categories: bulls and bears.

A bull is a speculator who takes an optimistic view of the future. He expects the price of a particular share to rise in the immediate future and, accordingly, buys shares at their current price in the hope of selling them later at a higher price. He is a speculator because he buys with the short-term objective of making quick profits out of price fluctuations. When a lot of bull activity dominates the stock market there is a general all-round rise in share prices. Such a market is commonly referred to as a bull market. Bull market thus is a term used to describe a rising market.

A bear, on the other hand, is a speculator who takes a pessimistic view of the future. He expects share prices to fall in the immediate future and seeks to make money by selling shares now in the hope of being able to buy them later at lower prices. Usually, he sells shares which he doesn't possess and expects that he can buy them later for delivery to the buyer. In stock market parlance, this is referred to as short selling. A bear is also a speculator because he hopes to make quick profits by taking advantage of a short-term fall in prices. A bear market is one which is characterised by a lot of bear activity. It is a term which is commonly used to describe a falling market.

Buyback of shares

Buyback of shares is a term that refers to a situation where a company buys back its own shares with its own capital.

A buyback of shares reduces the equity capital of a company. This happens because the shares bought back from the market are extinguished and cease to exist. The Company's Act debars the company from reissuing these shares again. As a result, not only does the equity capital reduce, but also the floating stock of the company's shares in the market shrinks to a lower level. Consequently the earnings per share (EPS) go up because the same amount of net post-tax earnings (as before the buyback) get spread over the reduced equity capital. As a consequence, the shares of the company get a better discounting, or P/E multiple, on the bourses and their price appreciates to a level that is considerably higher than the pre-buyback level.

Sometimes the buyback announcement indicates the company management's belief that the market has undervalued its shares and that they deserve a higher price. Such cases too result in a significant appreciation in the price of the company's shares, as a result of the great confidence in the value of its shares shown by its management.

Sometimes, company managements buy back their shares with a view to reducing the public holding in their company, as a step towards de-listing of their shares from the stock exchanges. When this happens, it usually has a dampening effect on the price of a company's shares. However, as a saving grace, shareholders do get ample opportunity to exit the company at better-than-market prices.

The buyback of shares by a company is usually announced at rates, which are higher, sometimes considerably higher, than their current quoted prices on the market. This gives investors an opportunity to make a windfall profit that they would not have got on the stock exchange under normal circumstances.

Stock splits

A stock split is completely different from a bonus issue of shares. A bonus issue of shares results in an increase in the equity capital of a company because through a book entry money is transferred from its reserves to its equity capital. In a stock split, the existing shares of the company are simply split into shares which have a smaller face value, or par value. Stock splits do not in any way increase or reduce the company's equity capital.

For example, let us take the stock split of XYZ Company whose shares have a par value of Rs. 10 per share. Suppose the company splits its Rs. 10 share into five shares with a par value of Rs. 2 each. If the pre-split price of the share was Rs. 5,000 and the stock is split five for one, then, theoretically speaking, the price of the new (split) share should be Rs. 1,000. The company's net assets or equity capital does not undergo any increase or decrease. A stock split benefits the investor because the share becomes cheaper in price. This invariably results in attracting more buyers with a consequent increase in liquidity and a proportionately higher post-split price. It has therefore been observed that the post-split price of the share that undergoes a stock split does not fall to its proportionate level compared to its pre-split price.

Take the case of Wipro whose shares with a par value of Rs. 10 per share were split into five shares with a par value of Rs. 2 each on 15 October 1999. It's pre-split price (after adjusting for the split) was around Rs. 1,284 per share, which, by 31 December 1999 had risen to Rs. 2,522 per share.

Dematerialization of shares

Dematerialization, as the name suggests, is a term used for conversion of shares from their physical form (physical share certificates) to the dematerialised or electronic form. After dematerialization, shares cease to exist in their physical, i.e. material, form. This conversion is done by the depository which also keeps custody of dematerialised shares on behalf of shareholders. There are two depositories in India; the CSDL (Central Securities Depository Limited) and the NSDL (National Securities Depository Limited). The CSDL acts as a depository for BSE, whereas the NSDL acts as a depository for the NSE.

To best understand what a depository is and how it functions, think of it as a bank. For all intents and purposes a depository is a securities bank which holds shares and bonds in the electronic form on behalf of its deposit holders just as your money held in normal bank is reflected as an entry in your pass book. It issues account holding statements and account transaction statements to its depositors in the same way that a bank does. A depository provides services to investors through its agents called Depository Participants (DPs). These DPs are mostly banks, financial institutions and brokers. Dealing with a depository participant in depositing and withdrawing your demat shares (an abbreviated form of dematerialised shares) is quite similar to operating a bank account.

Locating a depository participant in your city is not a major problem. The best course of action is to deal with the same DP as does your broker. This will make your share transactions easier and speedier. Also, in case any problem arises it would be easier for you and your broker to solve it since you would both be dealing with the same DP.

Dematerialization of shares with a DP involves a simple procedure. After opening a demat account with a DP, all you have to do is to surrender your physical share certificates, after cancelling them, to the DP along with a Demat Request Form (DRF). In the DRF you will be required to fill in all particulars of your shares, such as their folio numbers, distinctive numbers, share certificate numbers, etc. The DP then sends the DRF to the company, or its registrars and transfer agents, for conversion of the share certificates to their dematerialised, or electronic, form. After conversion they are credited to your account with the DP. This whole process of dematerialization normally takes about one month or so. For the detailed procedure of opening and operating a demat account and how to operate it, it would be advisable to consult your DP.

Rematerialization

Rematerialization is the reverse of dematerialization. It means converting shares held in the demat form back into physical share certificates. You have the complete freedom to re-convert your shares from the demat form to the physical form whenever you want. All you need to do is to request your DP for rematerialization of your shares. Your DP will forward your request to the depository. The depository will, in turn, intimate the concerned company, or its registrars and share transfer agents, who will send the required share certificates, bearing new folio numbers and distinctive numbers, back to you.

Advantages of dematerialization

The biggest advantage is that when you buy demat shares, you can rest assured that there is no risk of their being fake, forged or stolen shares as it sometimes happens with shares held in the physical form. Moreover, in the case of demat shares you need not worry about bad deliveries.

In the case of demat shares there is also no stamp duty on transfer of shares. Neither is there a complicated transfer form to fill up. As a result, an investor not only saves money but is also freed from the tedious and repetitive paperwork which invariably accompanies the buying and selling of shares in the physical form.

The stock exchanges have now discarded the earlier concept of marketable lots, small lots, and odd lots. This became possible only because of dematerialization of shares. Now even one share, no matter how small the denomination or how low the share price, can be bought or sold easily on the exchange. Demat is a big advantage for the small investor as it enables him to buy high-priced shares in small quantities which were earlier often out of his reach because a marketable lot of high-priced shares would usually involve a fairly large sum of money. Equally, demat enables the small investor to sell his odd lots and small lots of shares at market prices. Earlier, he would have been compelled to sell such lots at prices well below prevailing market price of the share.

Another big advantage of dematerialization of shares is that of nomination facility. This facility did not exist earlier in the case of physical share holdings; the law permits individuals to file a nomination form only in the case of a depository account. Even in the case of accounts held in joint names, the filing of nomination forms is permitted. In the event of the death of any one of the joint holders, the shares held in the joint account will be transferred to the single depository account of the surviving holder. If the surviving holder does not have a single account, then he will be required to open one in order to receive the shares earlier held in the joint depository account. The nominee would get the shares only in case all the joint holders die. Nomination facility is, however, not available to companies, Hindu Undivided Families, partnership firms, societies, trusts, etc.

In the case of dematerialised shares, change in your address no longer requires your having to send separate letters to each individual company whose shares you hold. All you need to do is to inform your DP of any change in your address, and the DP will send the new address to all the companies in which you hold shares. Your new address is then entered into the records of the company and the concerned depository.

In the case of dematerialised shares, bonus and rights shares are immediately transferred to your account with the DP as soon as they become due to you without any delay. When the shares are held in the physical form, the bonus/rights share certificates come through the post after a considerable delay which could be as long as three to four weeks. There is also the danger of their getting lost in transit, being mis-delivered by the postman, or otherwise falling into the wrong hands.

On-line trading

The earlier outcry system of auctions in the trading ring has now been replaced by the BOLT and NEAT systems. The BSE on-line trading system is called BOLT, whereas, the NSE has a similar system called NEAT. The purpose of these on-line trading systems is to provide an automated, computerised, all-India network platform for trading instantaneously, in real time. Through the BOLT and NEAT systems brokers can now enter orders on behalf of their clients from computer terminals installed in their offices instead of physically assembling in the trading ring. Trading is conducted from Monday to Friday between 9:55 a.m. and 3:30 p.m.

On-line trading has numerous advantages over the earlier system. To begin with it has neutralised the locational advantages of Mumbai *vis-à-vis* the rest of India. Any investor/trader who has access to a computer terminal which is hooked on to the BOLT or NEAT systems, is now placed on an equal footing with his counterpart in Mumbai. He does not suffer from any disadvantage arising from his geographical location.

It is now possible for an individual investor to place buy and sell orders through these on-line trading systems and watch them being instantaneously executed. This has resulted in a quantum leap in the volume of trading and in the liquidity of listed stocks.

On-line trading systems have also gone a long way in infusing greater confidence and trust amongst investors and traders. They can now actually watch their deals being executed exactly at the prices that they want. One of the main advantages of on-line trading systems is greater transparency in transactions.

Futures and options

The futures market came into existence in India in 2001 after the abolition of the traditional *badla* system. Futures and options are strictly for the experienced speculator or trader. We strongly advise the individual investor to steer clear of dabbling in futures and options. Nevertheless, we briefly describe below how the futures and options market works.

Futures

In your broker's office you will find a separate computer terminal devoted exclusively to futures and options. In the Indian stock markets, the cash market has been separated from the speculative (futures) market. In the cash market, unless you square off your deal on the same day, you have to make payment and take delivery of the shares that you buy. Similarly, in a sale transaction you have to give delivery and receive payment for the shares that you have sold. In the futures market, on the other hand, only the losses and gains made through buy and sale transactions are settled in cash there is physical delivery of shares.

So, how does this happen? The futures market deals with only a small number of shares selected by the exchange on the basis of liquidity, large floating stock, market capitalisation and volume of trading. A number of shares of the selected shares are grouped together in what is known as a contract. This contract is also known as a derivative. For example, suppose the contract size fixed for Hindustan Lever in the futures market is 1,000 shares. A trader can buy or sell only a contract, or multiple contracts, of Hindustan Lever. You cannot buy or sell Hindustan Lever futures in any other quantity.

In the futures market you do not have to pay for your purchase. You are only required to pay margin money, which may be 10 per cent to 20 per cent of the total value of the purchase. The amount of margin money that you have to pay on different contracts is fixed by the stock exchanges and varies from time to time depending on market conditions.

Currently, in the Indian markets you have the choice of buying contracts for one, two or three months, which you can square off any time you like before the expiry of the life of the contract. If you do not square off your contract, then the exchange compulsorily terminates your contract at the closing price on the last day of the life of the contract (usually the last Thursday of the month).

The attractiveness of the futures market lies in the fact that it allows a trader to leverage his capital; by paying margin money of say, Rs. 1 lakh, one could buy shares worth many times that amount. Leveraging is, however, a double-edged sword; while you could make huge gains, but you can also incur huge losses. In case you do want to trade in the futures market, then it would be advisable to use stop loss orders to minimise your losses. However, despite the use of stop loss orders, our practical experience has been that most investors tend to usually make big losses in the futures market.

Options

Options are another variation of futures trading. When you buy an option on a particular contract, you pay a premium for the right to buy/sell that contract at any price that gives you a profit, or minimises your losses, before the expiry of the contract. In case you do not exercise your option to terminate the contract, the maximum that you can lose is the amount that you paid as premium when you initially purchased the option. Buying options contract is a safer bet than futures. In the former the losses are limited to the premium that you have paid, whereas in the latter the losses have no limit.

The purchaser of options is at one end of the transaction, at the other end is the option writer. The option writer's risks are, in theory, limitless, whereas the liability of the purchaser of the option is limited to the premium amount paid at the time of purchase.

There are basically two types of options, the call option and the put option. Those who have taken a bullish view about the market, or the scrip that they intend to buy, normally buy call options. Whereas those who take a bearish view about the market, or the scrip that they intend buying, go in for put options.

Options trading is a highly complicated and tricky business. Its mastery requires a lot of experience. We would advise our readers to avoid it completely.

Fundamental analysis

Fundamental analysis is a term used to describe the approach some investors adopt for taking investment decisions. Persons who follow this approach are called fundamentalists. They try to estimate the intrinsic worth of a company's share by studying its sales, earnings, profits, dividends, management proficiency, and a host of other economic factors that have a bearing on the company's profitability and business prospects. They try to estimate what the price of a particular company's share ought to be, and consider this price to be its intrinsic, or true, value. This is called the intrinsic price of the share because it reflects its inherent worth and value. They then use it to judge whether the company's shares are currently over-priced or under-priced in the stock market.

The fundamentalist makes his money by buying under-priced shares and selling them when they later become over-priced.

Technical analysis

Technical analysis is another type of investment analysis commonly used for making buying and selling decisions in the stock market. It is an attempt to predict the future price of a particular share on the basis of a study of its price movements in the past. Technical analysts use charts and graphs for keeping a record of share price movements, which is why they are often referred to as chartists. They believe that a study of share price charts and graphs will reveal regular and recurrent patterns of price behaviour, which are likely to be repeated in the future. They use this knowledge to predict future price movements. After determining what future price movements are going to be like, they make money by appropriately timing their buying and selling of shares.

Technical analysts usually ignore all fundamental data, such as sales, earnings, profits, dividends, business prospects of the company, etc. They believe that these factors have already been taken into account by the market and are fully reflected in the current market price of a share.

By its very nature, technical analysis is particularly suitable for speculators and short-term traders in shares. It is difficult to take a long-term view on the basis of technical analysis. On the other hand, fundamental analysis is more useful for long-term investors. Since this book has been written for investors and not speculators, its overwhelming emphasis is on fundamental analysis.

Securities and Exchange Board of India (SEBI)

The Securities and Exchange Board of India (SEBI) is an autonomous body established by an Act of parliament in 1992. SEBI is controlled by a statutory board consisting of one chairman and six members. SEBI's main objective is to protect the interest of investors, and to regulate all securities markets in India. SEBI is a market regulator whose major functions include regulation, superintendence and control of all securities markets in India, overseeing the functioning of stock exchanges, framing rules for trading practices, attending to and removing investor grievances, framing rules for and regulating public issues, training and education of investors, and all matters pertaining to market intermediaries.

SEBI's address is given in Appendix A.

Stock market indices

The main purpose of a stock market index is to provide a means for measuring the overall trends in share prices in the market.

The stock market index is like an instrument that tracks the overall behaviour of the stock market. It is basically an average of a carefully selected portfolio that represents, or almost represents, the whole market. The shares selected for inclusion in the index generally have a high floating stock which is held by the public, high market capitalisation, high trading volumes, and high liquidity. The index is useful in that it gives you a quick fix on the market. If you want to know whether the market has gone up or down, or what the level of the market was one year ago, or five years ago, then all you have to do is to look at the movement of the index. You don't have to look at the price movements of each and every share listed on the market. The index, thus, represents the market.

The stock market index is also useful for comparing the returns you get from the stock markets with other assets, such as real estate, gold, collectibles, bonds, etc. Mutual funds use stock market indices for evaluating their portfolios. Some mutual funds have even floated index funds which mirror the composition of the index thus giving their investors returns similar to that of the index (*see* Chapter 12). This happened when it was found in U.S.A that most mutual funds tended to under-perform the index.

The most widely used stock market index in India is the BSE Sensitive Index, popularly known as Sensex. The BSE Sensitive Index was constructed in 1986, with 1978-79 as its base year. The value of Sensex in the base year was taken to be 100. Sensex is composed of 30 scrips selected on the basis of their size and daily trading volumes. Scrips are given weightage on the basis of their market capitalisation (number of equity shares multiplied by their share price). The index is therefore extremely sensitive to changes in the share prices of the larger companies.

The other widely used index in India is the S&P CNX Nifty Index, popularly known as Nifty. This is the main index of the

National Stock Exchange. The Nifty is composed of 50 stocks representing over 20 sectors of the economy, thus making it more broad-based and diversified than the Sensex. Nifty stocks account for 65 to 70 per cent of the traded volumes on NSE.

The shares comprising the Sensex and Nifty are listed in Appendix B. However, it must be remembered that the composition of the indices is changed quite frequently to reflect changes in the market capitalisation and volume of trading of the different scrips comprising on index. Thus, from time to time some scrips of an index are replaced with others. You can always find out which shares are included in the Sensex or Nifty from the BSE and NSE websites: www.bseindia.com and www.nseindia.com, respectively.

CHAPTER 3

How to buy and sell shares

Selecting a broker

When you decide to buy or sell shares, the first step to take is to choose a reliable broker or sub-broker who will carry out your transactions in a satisfactory manner. You can obtain a list of brokers and sub-brokers from the stock exchanges or from their websites. These addresses are given in Appendix A. You can go through these lists and tick mark the brokers/sub-brokers that, at first sight, appear to interest you.

A good broker will make it easier and more profitable for you to transact business on the stock exchange. Therefore it is important for you to put in the time and effort required in verifying the background of the broker or sub-broker with whom you intend to deal. It would be worthwhile to examine his track record, financial standing, and his local reputation in providing efficient services to his clients. Your more experienced and knowledgeable friends, business associates and other acquaintances are also a reliable source of information that you can tap for selecting a suitable broker or sub-broker.

Most investors are under the erroneous impression that their broker's job is to provide advice and tips on what to buy and sell. This could not be farther from the truth. There is a strong possibility that any advice coming from a broker could be biased and short-sighted. A broker's job is to execute your transaction for a fee and to provide you with all the necessary documentation.

Typically, he neither has the time, temperament nor the ability to give high-quality, research-based advice. Therefore do not be misled by brokers who promise to give you advice, insider information and timely tips.

Another important factor to consider is whether your broker or sub-broker encourages you to frequently churn your portfolio. Such brokers and sub-brokers are best avoided as their primary motivation is to increase their brokerage incomes through higher turnover of orders rather than looking after their client's interests.

A last bit of advice: deal only with a SEBI registered broker or sub-broker after making wide-ranging inquiries regarding his dealings with other clients and the quality and cost of the services that he provides.

How do you find out whether your stockbroker is reliable and sound? The only way to do so would be by actually dealing with him over a period of time. It is only through personal experience that you will really be able to assess what he is like.

Buying and selling shares

The first step is to open a demat account with your selected DP as explained in Chapter 2. All transactions on both the BSE and NSE are done in demat securities.

When you buy shares, you are required to pay money to your broker or sub-broker immediately upon getting the contract note/confirmation memo for the purchase of shares. The broker issues a contract note, whereas a sub-broker issues a confirmation memo. Similarly, when you sell shares you are required to give delivery of your shares by transferring them to the demat account of your broker/sub-broker immediately upon getting the contract note or confirmation memo. When you buy shares, then the shares you have purchased will first come to the demat account of your broker/sub-broker. Once this happens, you can instruct your broker/sub-broker to transfer those shares to your demat account. For receiving shares in your demat account you will have to give your broker or sub-broker the details regarding your demat account.

When you sell shares you are required to give delivery of shares from your demat account by instructing your DP to transfer the number of shares that you have sold from your account to the demat account of your broker. In this regard, you will be required to include the details of the demat account of your broker in the instruction slip that you give to your DP. Your broker or sub-broker will help you to fill in the delivery instructions. These instructions are of a technical nature and the delivery instruction forms and procedures differ from DP to DP.

How to place orders with the broker

The orders that you place with your broker or sub-broker would mainly be of three kinds:

1. Fixed price order, or limit order;
2. Stop loss order; or
3. Market order.

A **fixed price** order is one when you want to execute your trade (purchase or sale) at a fixed price. In practice, investors normally place a fixed price order at a price that is a little higher or a little lower than the current price shown on the screen. The fixed price order is better than a market order in that it removes the price uncertainty associated with your buy or sell order. Fixed price orders are suitable for executing large orders and for buying and selling shares that are relatively illiquid. Fixed price orders are also useful if you want to buy or sell your shares at a predetermined price.

A **stop loss order** is one which is placed at a fixed price along with a trigger price in your broker or sub-broker's computer. Once the market price reaches the trigger price, your order gets activated. This stop loss order and its linked trigger price has to be higher or lower than the current market price at the time of placing the order. As soon as a trade takes place in the market at the trigger price, then the order, whether a buy or sell order, gets activated in the system. Suppose you purchase shares of Hind Lever at Rs. 100 per share. Further suppose that you are not sure of which way the share will move, but you would like to limit your losses to Rs. 10 per share. Then you can feed in your stop loss order, which is a sell order, at Rs. 90 per share with the trigger price of Rs. 91 per share. When the share price falls to Rs. 91 per share, the stop loss order is automatically activated. However, your order will be executed at only Rs. 90 per share. Similarly, a stop loss order can be placed with respect to a share that you have sold, but which you may want to buy back at a lower price.

Traders and speculators who would like to limit their losses, or take their profits at pre-fixed levels, mostly use stop loss orders. Here are some of the typical situations where you may wish to use a stop loss order:

- Suppose you are a trader who has taken a buy or sell position and would like to protect yourself in case the market moves in the reverse direction. You can then use a stop loss order to limit your losses.
- Stop loss orders are also useful for traders who have taken a sale or a buy position but don't have the time or the inclination to keep track of the share price movements.
- Stop loss orders are useful if you would like to buy or sell a stock only after it crosses a certain pre-fixed price level that you have in mind because your technical study of charts reveals that an uptrend or downtrend is likely to be activated after it crosses this particular price level. Momentum traders often use this technique. Their study reveals that the share price is likely to gather momentum after it crosses a pre-fixed level.

A **market order** is one where you want to execute your trade (purchase or sale) at the market price shown on the broker/sub-broker's computer screen. Suppose you want to buy 100 shares of XYZ Company, and you place a market order for the same. Further suppose that the computer screen shows that there are sellers for 80 shares only at the market price of, say Rs. 60 per share. Also suppose that the next lot of sellers are quoting at a price of Rs. 62 per share. Then your order will be executed in the following manner: 80 shares will be bought at Rs. 60 per share, and the remaining 20 shares at Rs. 62 per share. In a wildly fluctuating market, or in the case of stocks where the liquidity is low, one should not use a market order. A market order should be used only when you want to buy or sell a particular stock in a hurry and where you are not unduly bothered about the price at which your trade is executed. A market order should also not be used when you are placing a large order.

Preliminary paperwork

When you start dealing with a broker there will be two account-opening forms that you will be required to fill:

1. Client introductory form; and
2. Broker client agreement.

Your broker will help you fill in these forms. You will be required to give details, such as your name, address, income tax PAN number, photo identity documents, details of your bank account, proof of residence, etc. The broker client agreement and the client introductory form have been drawn up by SEBI and have a standardised format. Our only advice is to carefully read and understand these documents before signing any of them.

CHAPTER 4

Three basic investment rules

Rule 1: Don't buy unlisted shares

There are over 20,000 public limited companies in India, of which only around 7,000 are listed on the country's various stock exchanges. The first rule of profitable share investment is to confine your buying to these 7,000 listed companies only.

Stock exchanges do not permit trading in unlisted shares, nor do they permit their registered members, i.e. brokers to deal in unlisted shares. Therefore, if you want to buy unlisted shares you won't get the protection of the stock exchange authorities; nor will you be able to use the services of your stockbroker in handling such transactions. Moreover, in the absence of stock exchange quotations you won't be able to assess what the market price of an unlisted share should be. All these factors create complications and risks, which you are not likely to be in a position to handle. As a basic rule, therefore, you should avoid investing in shares of unlisted companies.

As a basic rule you should avoid investing in shares of unlisted companies.

How does one know whether a share is listed or not? It's simple; all shares whose prices are quoted in daily newspapers are listed shares. Unlisted shares are never quoted. Therefore, the fact that a share is quoted means that it must be listed. This is the easiest and surest way of finding out whether a particular share is listed or not.

Rule 2: Don't buy inactive shares

Active shares are those in which transactions take place every day, or almost every day, on the stock exchange. At the other extreme are shares in which transactions take place rarely, if ever. The latter are called inactive shares. In this book, an inactive share has been defined as one which is transacted less than two times a month, or not at all.

The main reason why shares are inactive is because there are no buyers for them. They are mostly shares of companies which are not doing well and whose future prospects appear to be dim. Naturally, nobody wants to buy their shares. As a result, existing shareholders of these companies find it difficult to get rid of their shares, even at very low prices. And, if nobody wants to buy these shares, why should you? Why should you allow yourself to get stuck with an investment, which you can't offload at will, whenever you want to? We would strongly advise you to avoid investing in inactive shares.

How does one find out whether a particular share is inactive or not? The simplest way is to regularly scrutinise the stock market quotations which appear in the daily newspapers. If you find that a particular share has not been quoted for a long time, you can presume it is inactive. Some newspapers, like *The Financial Express* not only indicate the last quoted price of each share, but also the date when it was last transacted. This information can help you to confirm whether a particular share is inactive.

Inactive shares can generally be bought at very low prices. This is obvious since such shares generally find no buyers. Inexperienced investors looking for bargains are often attracted to such shares by virtue of their low prices. This is how beginners are normally trapped into making disastrous investments. Beware of such bargains! If you come across a bargain, remember there has to be a catch in it somewhere. It is better to hunt for value, and pay a fair price for it, than to look for such apparent bargains.

Every time you buy a share, you must remember that one day you will want to sell it. If you think you are likely to face difficulty in selling it — don't buy it! This is a sound investment principle which you should never lose sight of, no matter how cheap or attractive a particular investment may appear to be. Never allow yourself to get caught with illiquid shares. They are only pieces of paper without any value. Shares have value only when they are readily encashable.

Of course, it is possible that a share which is inactive today could become active tomorrow; just as a share which is active today could become inactive tomorrow. It all depends upon the degree of buying interest in a particular share. If buying interest builds up in a share, it can easily move from the inactive to the active category.

Rule 3: Don't buy shares in closely held companies

Whether a company is widely held or closely held depends upon the number of shareholders it has. In this book, we will draw the line at 5,000 shareholders. Companies with less than 5,000 shareholders will be considered as closely held.

Shares of closely held companies tend to be less active than those of widely held ones since they have a fewer number of shareholders and, thus, a smaller floating stock of shares. Shares of such companies tend to be ignored by the general public. Large institutional investors also tend to avoid closely held companies. As a result their shares do not get sufficient price support, which they would otherwise have got if they had been widely held. Moreover, it is always much easier to manipulate the share prices of a closely held company than those of a widely held one.

Share prices of closely held companies also tend to be more volatile than others. When they rise they rise very fast, and to a very high level. Conversely, when they fall they do so very fast and to a very low level. As a result, it is generally very difficult to buy shares in a closely held company when prices are rising, and very difficult to sell them when prices are falling. Investing in such shares requires a high degree of expertise, knowledge, alertness and quick thinking which take years of active investing to acquire. We would, therefore, strongly urge you to keep away from such shares.

CHAPTER 5

What to look for in a company

Is the management dynamic and forward looking?

A company can only be as good, or as bad, as its management. It is management that provides the main driving force behind corporate performance. Therefore, as a would-be investor it is necessary for you to find out the quality of a company's management before you invest in its shares.

To begin with, don't be misled by commonplace cliches which most people use to judge company managements by, such as family managements are bad, professional managements are good, or foreign managements are good, others are not so good, etc. Companies run by traditional business families can sometimes be as dynamic and forward-looking as the best of professionally run subsidiaries of foreign multinationals. On the other hand, some foreign companies with so-called professional managements have a poor record of performance. Therefore, don't go merely by labels; look, instead, for the real picture.

One way to find out whether a management is good or bad is to look at its past performance. Look at its track record. Look at what its growth rate has been in the past. Growth rate can be judged by looking at a company's sales, profits and gross block over the last three to five years. Find out how it has fared as compared to companies of a similar size engaged in similar operations. How has the company coped in the past with adverse business conditions, like a demand recession, rising costs, etc.? Has the management shown awareness of future business conditions and changing trends in business and industry? If so, then what has it done to deal with, or take advantage of them? Has the company tried to keep up with the times by replacing obsolete equipment and introducing technological innovations, new products and designs, and by adopting new and more effective management practices, etc? The answers to these questions will help you decide whether a particular company's management is sufficiently dynamic for you to invest in it.

How does one go about getting the information necessary for probing into the quality of a particular company's management? Most newspapers and magazines — particularly the financial dailies and business magazines (list given in Appendix A) — give a lot of coverage to news concerning prominent companies and their managements. Most of these articles are analytical and probing and can provide you with valuable insight into the functioning and performance of different company managements.

Sometimes you will come across companies whose managements are riven with factionalism and infighting. These managements will not have the necessary unity of purpose, loyalty, or the cohesiveness required for high quality corporate performance. You should therefore avoid investing in such companies, unless you have strong reasons to believe that such factionalism and infighting are purely temporary and will soon give way to a responsible and united management.

Is the company sufficiently large in size?

Large companies generally offer better investment opportunities than do smaller ones. This is because large companies can make use of economies of scale which smaller companies cannot. The former are thus able to reduce costs and establish a clear competitive edge over smaller companies. Since their costs are lower, they can cope more effectively with adverse economic and business conditions. During a prolonged business crisis, small companies are generally the first to run up large losses and down their shutters. This is the main reason behind the high incidence of failure amongst mini steel plants and mini paper mills during the last few years.

Large companies also generally pay higher salaries and offer better working conditions to their managers and staff. So they are able to attract better qualified and talented personnel than can smaller companies and, as a result, are likely to be better managed and more efficient. By virtue of their higher production, large companies generally occupy a stronger and more dominant position in the market. Since larger companies normally generate larger surpluses, they can spend more on research and development, marketing, expansion and diversification programmes.

As a result, investment in large companies is generally safer and more stable than in smaller companies. However, this does not mean you should ignore small companies altogether. In recent years, there have been a number of cases where relatively small companies have performed spectacularly well and rewarded their shareholders generously with steep capital appreciation and high dividends. Arvind Mills, HEG, Hikal, Matrix Laboratories are a few such companies. Though investments in smaller companies sometimes give spectacular returns, you must note that for every such company there are many more in number which have been miserable failures. As a beginner you are likely to do much better if you confine your investments to large companies where the incidence of failure is lower. Later, when you acquire more knowledge and experience, you can venture into investing in smaller companies which you think are likely to do well.

As a beginner you are likely to do much better if you confine your investments to large companies where the incidence of failure is lower.

Table 5.1

Some of the largest companies in India

1.	State Bank of India	7.	ACC
2.	Tata Steel	8.	ONGC
3.	ITC Ltd.	9.	Hindalco
4.	Reliance Industries	10.	Tata Motors
5.	Hindustan Lever	11.	SAIL
6.	TELCO	12.	L & T.

How does one decide whether a company is large or small? Where does one draw the dividing line? Again, though there is no rigid and universally applicable rule in this regard, we would suggest that as a rule-of-thumb companies with an equity capital of less than Rs. 10 crore and sales of less than Rs. 50 crore could be considered very small and by and large, you should avoid investing in such companies.*

Does the company have a core competence or is it diversified?

Diversification in a company can take many forms. The most obvious forms are a diversified product range and diversified business operations. For example, a company like Hindustan Lever has a diversified range of products, comprising soaps, detergents, toothpastes, fertilisers and agro-chemicals. Larsen & Turbo, on the other hand, has a diversified range of business operations, including cement, manufacturing, construction and consultancy. Diversification can also be achieved through geographical dispersal of factories and markets. This protects the company from natural calamities, like floods, earthquakes, etc. which occur only in particular parts of the country and therefore can, at worst, affect only a part of the company's operations. Some companies diversify their markets by selling their products in both domestic

---

* *Capital Market* gives a very comprehensive database on 2,000 listed companies, which will enable you to judge the size of companies.

and foreign markets. In fact, there are numerous ways in which companies achieve diversification.

Companies that are industry leaders by virtue of their core competence generally make better investments than large diversified companies.

Most companies these days have shed diversification into unrelated businesses in favour of concentration on their areas of core competence. They have either sold off their less profitable businesses, or outsourced all business activities other than the one in which they have inherent strengths. For example, Hindustan Lever has been systematically selling all its manufacturing units and its less profitable brands and concentrating only on what its board refers to as power brands. L&T is demerging its cement unit. It has been reported in newspapers that Raymond is thinking of selling its steel unit. Companies that are industry leaders by virtue of their core competence generally make better investments than large diversified companies. The former tend to be cost efficient, dynamic and register faster growth than do diversified companies, which by and large tend to be slow and sluggish.

An investor can achieve diversification in many ways. The most obvious way is to invest in a number of well-diversified companies. However, a better way to achieve diversification is to invest in a number of companies that by virtue of concentration on core competence have become industry leaders in their respective fields. Diversification of your portfolio is a compulsion that you cannot ignore irrespective of the manner in which you achieve it. Diversification not only provides safety and stability to your portfolio, it also provides you with the necessary flexibility in dealing with changing business conditions.

Companies that have concentrated on their area of core competence are, no doubt, risky investments. However, if your portfolio consists of a basket of such companies operating in different

Table 5.2

Some well-known diversified companies

1. Grasim Industries	6. Larsen & Turbo
2. Hindustan Lever	7. ICI (India)
3. ITC	8. Reliance Industries
4. Indian Rayon	9. Apollo Hospitals
5. Nestle	10. WIPRO

Table 5.3

Some well-known companies with concentrated businesses

1. Hero Honda	6. Nalco
2. Bharat Forge	7. Motherson Sumi
3. Gujarat Amb. Cement	8. Balrampur Chini
4. Infosys Technologies	9. ABB
5. Indian Hotels	10. Essel Propack

industries and in different sectors of the economy, then your risks are amply covered. Moreover, under favourable conditions these companies perform extremely well — often far better than do widely diversified companies. It is only under adverse business conditions that their weaknesses are exposed. As a general rule, you should avoid investing in any company that is concentrated in a single business area unless it falls in one of the following three categories:

1. Companies whose products enjoy a monopoly or a near-monopoly in the market;
2. Companies, with a captive and growing market for their products; and
3. Companies which, for one reason or another, hold a dominant position in their respective fields *vis-a-vis* their nearest competitors.

Is it a growth company?

Growth companies provide excellent investment opportunities. As a company grows and expands, so will its profits. This means not only liberal and frequent bonus issues in the future but also continuously rising dividends. This is the main reason why growth companies are eagerly sought after by investors. In fact, it would not be much of an exaggeration to suggest that the search for, and identification of, growth companies dominates all investment activity.

How does one identify a growth company? One of the simplest ways of doing so is to look at the company's record of performance. Companies that have a proven record of growth in the past are the ones which are most likely to grow in the future. This is not always true but it does explain to a great extent the consistency with which most growth companies tend to maintain their pace of growth while others don't. The fact that a company has an excellent record of growth implies that it has a dynamic, growth-oriented management. Management policies don't change overnight. A management that is growth-oriented is likely to continue to remain so in the future also.

Growth companies will generally be found in growing industries, and growing sectors or areas of the economy. Only very rarely will you find a growth company in a stagnant or declining sector of the economy.

Growth companies will generally be found in growing industries, and growing sectors or areas of the economy. Only very rarely will you find a growth company in a stagnant or declining sector of the economy. Even if you do, the growth prospects of such a company are bound to be short-lived and limited. Therefore, if you want to locate growth companies you must first identify the growth areas of the economy. Once you do this, it will not be difficult to identify companies that will probably step in and take advantage of these.

One way to recognise a growth situation is to foresee the future demand for any product or product-group. How this is done can best be illustrated by taking a real life situation.

For example, everybody is aware of the growing need for quality healthcare. Increase in longevity of life, entry of private sector health insurance companies, virtual breakdown of healthcare services in USA and Europe, paucity of corporate hospitals, and poor quality of healthcare facilities in government run hospitals has created ideal conditions for the rapid growth of the healthcare sector in India. In fact, healthcare is the fastest growing sector worldwide with an estimated annual growth rate of around 24 per cent. The implementation of the WTO accord after 31 December 2004 opens up rapid growth opportunities in pharmaceuticals, textiles, farm produce and IT services.

Another growth area is commodities. Commodities, like aluminium, steel, copper, have just emerged from a 30-year bear market. Burgeoning demand from China and high GDP growth rates in Asia, particularly India, have opened up attractive growth opportunities in commodities.

Then, too, every day we read in newspapers about the growing rate of urbanisation and the rapidly increasing number of working couples in urban areas. These two broad trends present a growth situation. If these trends continue, you can foresee the future implications. Let us try to see what these could possibly be. Working couples mean a change in consumer and food habits. When the husband and wife come home in the evening after a long and tiring day at work, they won't have the time, energy, or inclination to do time consuming and strenuous domestic chores. The answer to their problems lies in easy-to-cook, processed or semi-processed foods, a switch from cotton fabrics to easy-to-maintain clothes made from synthetic materials, easily available home entertainment, time- and energy-saving gadgets like pressure cookers, washing machines, refrigerators, etc. Moreover, the

Table 5.4

Some growth companies in India

1. ABB Ltd.	7. Indian Hotels
2. Bajaj Auto	8. Indian Rayon
3. Siemen	9. Infosys Technologies
4. TISCO	10. Larsen & Turbo
5. Gujarat Ambuja Cement	11. Reliance Industries
6. Wipro	12. TELCO

availability of two incomes in the family instead of one income, means that the couple will have the necessary purchasing power for switching over to a new lifestyle. This is a growth situation for companies producing refrigerators, pressure cookers, home appliances, processed foods, television sets, videos and personal care items. A working wife will also insist on spending a part of her own income on toiletries, cosmetics and personal care products.

Growth doesn't come by accident — companies have to plan for growth. They have to identify growth products and areas and prepare detailed plans for implementation of expansion-cum-diversification projects. They have to make arrangements for the financing of these projects, buy land, sign foreign collaboration agreements for import of technical know-how and equipment, and obtain clearances from concerned government agencies. All these activities get a lot of press coverage and publicity. If you are alert and make it a point to read financial newspaper carefully, it should not be difficult to get information on companies that are gearing up for future growth. If you invest in the shares of a company that is about to embark upon a major growth phase then you can make a fair amount of money by the time this growth phase reaches its peak. A basic point that you should keep in mind is that the future of your investment in any company is directly linked with the performance of that company. If the company grows, so will your investment — in fact, sometimes the rate at which your investment grows may outstrip the company's growth rate. This usually happens when investors in their enthusiasm over a company's growth prospects push up its share prices to unjustifiably high levels, thus offering opportunities to smart investors to sell their shares at a handsome profit.

The company's environment

Companies are inextricably linked to their industrial, commercial and economic environments. They can't hope to isolate themselves from these environmental influences. In an adverse environment, even the most profitable and well managed companies find the going tough, whereas a favourable environment usually gives a boost to even the most sluggish and mismanaged companies. Therefore, if you want to accurately assess a company's business prospects you must take its environment into account.

Like every other free-market economy, India's economy is subject to cyclical swings between periods of boom and recession. Since the Indian economy is dominated by agriculture, a steep rise in agricultural production invariably leads to an industrial boom, whereas a fall in agricultural production is usually followed by a general all-round recession in the economy. Agricultural production is, in turn, heavily dependent upon the success or failure of the monsoon. As an investor, therefore, you should not only keep a tab on agricultural production figures but also on rainfall and monsoon forecasts. This will enable you to not only anticipate periods of boom and recession, but also to profit from them through timely and appropriate investments. The sales and profits of most companies rise during a boom and fall during a recession. It is only occasionally that one comes across a company whose performance moves against the general trend. Therefore, you should try to find out whether the company you are interested in is one which moves with the trend or against it. Also, find out the extent to which the company is influenced by a boom or recession in the economy.

Inflation is a persistent and nation-wide problem which affects the working and performance of all companies. However, the nature and extent of its impact on each company varies considerably. Some companies are adversely affected by it, whereas others are not only able to effectively cope with inflation, but actually thrive on it. For example, companies manufacturing mopeds have actually grown and prospered as a direct result of inflation. This is because an increase in the cost of living, particularly the cost of transport, forces many to switch over from cars, scooters and motorcycles to mopeds. Inflation usually pushes up the costs of production. Some companies can pass on this increase in costs to consumers while others cannot. The former benefit from inflation, while the latter are adversely affected by it. Inflation redistributes purchasing power within the economy. This leads to a contraction in demand for some products and an expansion in the demand for others. Some companies benefit from this, others don't. These are some of the obvious ways in which inflation affects the working and performance of companies.

The performance of the railways, power plants and the coal, oil and steel industries are major environmental factors, which have a widespread impact upon the performance of all companies. As an investor, therefore, you should try and determine the extent to which a company that you are interested in is likely to be affected by shortages in the availability of coal, power, railway wagons, oil and steel. In addition, what impact would a rise in railway freight rates, power tariffs, or a rise in the price of steel, coal and oil have on the company's profits?

Corporate performances are also extremely sensitive to changes in interest rates, excise and customs duties, depreciation rates, import-export policies and the exchange rate of the rupee *vis-a-vis* other major international currencies. It would be useful for you to find out to what extent the performance of the company you want to invest in is likely to be influenced by these factors. A strong rupee and falling customs duties could create an adverse operating environment for companies that cannot compete with cheap imports. Historically, low interest rates have been known to benefit companies operating in the transport, construction and agricultural equipment industries. Leasing and hire purchase companies also benefit immensely from falling interest rates.

Does the company have labour problems?

Most companies, at some time or other, face labour problems. However, in most cases these problems are not very serious and they do not really disrupt the functioning of the company in a major way. The companies to avoid are those which have a long and violent history of strained management-labour relations. In such companies, production is frequently disrupted, sometimes over prolonged periods of time. The Bombay textile strike in the early 1980s showed how a prolonged and violent labour agitation ruined the Bombay textile industry. We would advise you to keep away from companies suffering from chronic labour problems, and those which are located in areas where labour agitation has become endemic.

Is the company internationally competitive?

The Indian economy is now getting integrated with the world economy. This process of integration is expected to be completed by 31 December 2004. The WTO (World Trade Organisation) agreement also provides for the integration of the economies of member countries through lowering of tariff barriers, reductions in subsidies, greater protection for patents and copyrights, and the gradual removal of restrictions on free movement of goods, services and personnel across nations. In such an environment only those companies that are in a position to compete in the global markets, or against cheap imports coming into their domestic markets, can possibly hope to survive and grow.

How do you identify an internationally competitive company? One way to do so would be to take a look at the volume and nature of a company's exports. The very fact that a company can get export orders and sell its products in international markets, particularly in advanced markets like those of USA, Europe or Japan, means that the company is internationally competitive. Indian companies belonging to the following industries are, by and large, internationally competitive because India enjoys a comparative advantage in these industries:

- IT services,
- Healthcare,
- Silk,
- Cotton textiles,
- Floriculture,
- Fruits,
- Milk products,
- Two-wheelers,
- Pharmaceuticals,
- Tea,
- Leather products,
- Mushrooms,
- Poultry products,
- Vegetables,
- Auto ancillaries,
- Gems, and Jewellery.

Companies that for one reason or another are naturally immune from international competition can also look forward to a bright future since they have virtually unlimited growth opportunities in the vast Indian domestic market. Cement companies belong to this category. The high cost of transportation of cement insulates domestic cement companies from cheap imports and unless a foreign cement company sets up manufacturing facilities in India, it cannot offer any competition to an Indian cement company. Hotels, by virtue of their locational advantages, are also protected from competition from similar hotels located in other cities. Power generating and distributing companies also face no international competition.

On the other hand, by virtue of their high costs of production companies manufacturing fertilisers, consumer durables, electronic products, petrochemicals and petrochemical intermediates, will find their profit margins threatened in a regime of low tariff barriers.

Taking a global view, India's main economic strengths lie in its vast and productive land surface, a long coastline, a large variety of agro-climatic conditions, a huge population, low labour costs, and a vast pool of cheap but highly trained and resourceful technical and managerial manpower. India is also endowed with vast mineral resources and is self-sufficient in about 40 minerals which provide the primary raw materials for core sectors, like power, coal, steel, ferro alloys, aluminium, cement, zinc, refractories and chemicals. What India lacks is oil, sulphur, asbestos, rock phosphate, potash, copper, lead, tungsten and nickel. Companies that can utilise these unique strengths of India to advantage should be able to reward their shareholders with generous profits in the years to come.

CHAPTER 6

How to select a company to invest in

Ploughback and reserves

After deduction of all expenses including taxes, the net profits of a company are split into two parts — dividends and ploughback. Dividend is that portion of a company's profits which is distributed to its shareholders, whereas ploughback is the portion that the company retains and gets added to its reserves. The figures for ploughback and reserves of any company can be obtained by a cursory glance at its balance sheet and profit and loss account. Most newspapers and business and investment magazines also give this information for prominent companies while reporting their annual working results.

It is important to compare the size of a company's reserves with the size of its equity capital. This will indicate whether the company is in a position to issue bonus shares.

Ploughback is important because it not only increases the reserves of a company but also provides the company with funds required for its growth and expansion. All growth companies maintain a high level of ploughback. So if you are looking for a growth company to invest in, you should examine its ploughback figures. Companies that have no intention of expanding are unlikely to ploughback a large portion of their profits.

Reserves constitute the accumulated retained profits of a company. It is important to compare the size of a company's reserves with the size of its equity capital. This will indicate whether the company is in a position to issue bonus shares. As a rule-of-thumb, a company whose reserves are double that of its equity capital should be in a position to make a liberal bonus issue.

Retained profits also belong to the shareholders. This is why reserves are often referred to as shareholders' funds. Therefore, any addition to the reserves of a company will normally lead to a corresponding an increase in the price of your shares. The higher the reserves, the greater will be the value of your shareholding. Retained profits (ploughback) may not come to you in the form of cash, but they benefit you by pushing up the price of your shares.

Book value per share

You will come across this term very often in investment literature. Book value per share indicates what each share of a company is worth according to the company's books of accounts. The company's books of account maintain a record of what the company owns (assets), and what it owes to its creditors (liabilities). If you subtract the total liabilities of a company from its total assets, then what is left belongs to the shareholders, called the shareholders' funds. If you divide shareholders' funds by the total number of equity shares issued by the company, the figure that you get will be the book value per share.

$$\text{Book Value Per Share} = \frac{\text{Shareholders' Funds}}{\text{Total Number of Equity Shares Issued}}$$

The figure for shareholders' funds can also be obtained by adding the equity capital and reserves of the company.

Book value is a historical record based on the original prices at which assets of the company were first purchased. It doesn't reflect the current market value of the company's assets. Therefore, book value per share has limited usage as a tool for evaluating the market value or price of a company's shares. It can, at best, give you a rough idea of what a company's shares should be worth.

The market prices of shares are generally much higher than what their book values indicate. Therefore, if you come across a share whose market price is around its book value, the chances are that it is under-priced. This is one way in which the book value per share ratio can prove useful to you while assessing whether a particular share is over- or under-priced.

Earnings per share (EPS)

EPS is a well-known and widely used investment ratio. It is calculated as:

$$\text{Earnings Per Share (EPS)} = \frac{\text{Profit After Tax}}{\text{Total Number of Equity Shares Issued}}$$

This ratio gives the earnings of a company on a per share basis. In order to get a clear idea of what this ratio signifies, let us assume that you possess 100 shares with a face value of Rs. 10 each in XYZ Ltd. Suppose the earnings per share of XYZ Ltd. is Rs. 6 per share and the dividend declared by it is 20 per cent, or Rs. 2 per share. This means that each share of XYZ Ltd. earns Rs. 6 every year, even though you receive only Rs. 2 out of it as dividend. The remaining amount, Rs. 4 per share, constitutes the ploughback or retained earnings. If you had bought these shares at par, it would mean a 60 per cent return on your investment, out of which you would receive 20 per cent as dividend and 40 per cent would be the ploughback. This ploughback of 40 per cent would benefit you by pushing up the market price of your shares. Ideally speaking, your shares should appreciate by 40 per cent from Rs. 10 to Rs. 14 per share.

This illustration serves to drive home a basic investment lesson. You should evaluate your investment returns not on the basis of the dividend you receive, but on the basis of the earnings per share. Earnings per share is the true indicator of the returns on your share investments.

Suppose you had bought shares in XYZ Ltd at double their face value, i.e. at Rs. 20 per share. Then an EPS of Rs. 6 per share would mean a 30 per cent return on your investment, of which 10 per cent (Rs. 2 per share) is dividend, and 20 per cent (Rs. 4 per share) the ploughback. Under ideal conditions, ploughback should push up the price of your shares by 20 per cent, i.e. from Rs. 20 to 24 per share. Therefore, irrespective of what price you buy a particular company's shares at its EPS will provide you with an invaluable tool for calculating the returns on your investment.

You should evaluate your investment returns not on the basis of the dividend you receive, but on the basis of the earnings per share. Earnings per share is the true indicator of the returns on your share investments.

Price earnings ratio (P/E)

The price earnings ratio (P/E) expresses the relationship between the market price of a company's share and its earnings per share:

$$\text{Price/Earnings Ratio (P/E)} = \frac{\text{Price of the Share}}{\text{Earnings per Share}}$$

This ratio indicates the extent to which earnings of a share are covered by its price. If P/E is 5, it means that the price of a share is 5 times its earnings. In other words, the company's EPS remaining constant, it will take you approximately five years through dividends plus capital appreciation to recover the cost of buying the share. The lower the P/E, lesser the time it will take for you to recover your investment.

P/E ratio is a reflection of the market's opinion of the earnings capacity and future business prospects of a company. Companies which enjoy the confidence of investors and have a higher market standing usually command high P/E ratios. For example, blue chip companies often have P/E ratios that are as high as 20 to

60. However, most other companies in India have P/E ratios ranging between 5 and 20.

On the face of it, it would seem that companies with low P/E ratios would offer the most attractive investment opportunities. This is not always true. Companies with high current earnings but dim future prospects often have low P/E ratios. Obviously such companies are not good investments, not-withstanding their P/E ratios. As an investor your primary concern is with the future prospects of a company and not so much with its present performance. This is the main reason why companies with low current earnings but bright future prospects usually command high P/E ratios. To a great extent, the present price of a share, discounts, i.e. anticipates, its future earnings.

All this may seem very perplexing to you because it leaves the basic question unanswered: How does one use the P/E ratio for making sound investment decisions?

The answer lies in utilising the P/E ratio in conjunction with your assessment of the future earnings and growth prospects of a company. You have to judge the extent to which its P/E ratio reflects the company's future prospects. If it is low compared to the future prospects of a company, then the company's shares are good for investment. Therefore, even if you come across a company with a high P/E ratio of 25 or 30 don't summarily reject it because even this level of P/E ratio may actually be low if the company is poised for meteoric future growth. On the other hand, a low P/E ratio of 4 or 5 may actually be high if your assessment of the company's future indicates sharply declining sales and large losses.

Dividend and yield

There are many investors who buy shares with the objective of earning a regular income from their investment. Their primary concern is with the amount that a company gives as dividends —

capital appreciation being only a secondary consideration. For such investors, dividends obviously play a crucial role in their investment calculations.

It is illogical to draw a distinction between capital appreciation and dividends. Money is money — it doesn't really matter whether it comes from capital appreciation or from dividends. A wise investor is primarily concerned with the total returns on his investment — he doesn't really care whether these returns come from capital appreciation or dividends, or through varying combinations of both. In fact, investors in high tax brackets prefer to get most of their returns through long-term capital appreciation because of tax considerations.

Companies that give high dividends not only have a poor growth record but often also poor future growth prospects. If a company distributes the bulk of its earnings in the form of dividends, there will not be enough ploughback for financing future growth. On the other hand, high growth companies generally have a poor dividend record. This is because such companies use only a relatively small proportion of their earnings to pay dividends. In the long run, however, high growth companies not only offer steep capital appreciation but also end up paying higher dividends. On the whole, therefore, you are likely to get much higher total returns on your investment if you invest for capital appreciation rather than for dividends. In short, it all boils down to whether you are prepared to sacrifice a part of your immediate dividend income in the expectation of greater capital appreciation and higher dividends in the years to come and the whole issue is basically a trade-off between capital appreciation and income.

You are likely to get much higher total returns on your investment if you invest for capital appreciation rather than for dividends.

Investors are not really interested in dividends but in the relationship that dividends bear to the market price of the company's shares. This relationship is best expressed by the ratio called yield or dividend yield:

$$\text{Yield} = \frac{\text{Dividend per Share}}{\text{Market Price per Share}} \times 100$$

Yield indicates the percentage of return that you can expect by way of dividends on your investment made at the prevailing market price. The concept of yield is best clarified by the following illustration.

Let us suppose you have invested Rs. 2,000 in buying 100 shares of XYZ Ltd at Rs. 20 per share with a face value of Rs. 10 each. If XYZ announces a dividend of 20 per cent (Rs. 2 per share), then you stand to get a total dividend of Rs. 200. Since you bought these shares at Rs. 20 per share, the yield on your investment is 10 per cent (Yield = 2/20 x 100). Thus, while the dividend was 20 per cent; but your yield is actually 10 per cent.

The concept of yield is of far greater practical utility than dividends. It gives you an idea of what you are earning through dividends on the current market price of your shares. Average yield figures in India usually vary around 2 per cent of the market value of the shares. If you have a share portfolio consisting of shares belonging to a large number of both high-growth and high-dividend companies, then on an average your dividend income is likely to be around 2 per cent of the total market value of your portfolio.

ROCE, RONW and PEG ratios

While analysing a company, the most important thing you would like to know is whether the company is efficiently using the capital (shareholders' funds plus borrowed funds) entrusted to it.

While valuing the efficiency and worth of companies, we need to know the return that a company is able to earn on its capital, namely its equity plus debt. Those companies that earn a higher return on the capital it employs are more valuable than those which earn a lower return on their capital. The tools for measuring these returns are:

1. Return on Capital Employed (ROCE), and
2. Return on Net Worth (RONW).

Return on Capital Employed and Return on Net Worth (shareholders funds) are valuable financial ratios for evaluating a company's efficiency and the quality of its management. The figures for these ratios are commonly available in business magazines (especially in *Capital Market*), annual reports and economic newspapers and financial websites.

A company raises its capital from two sources, namely debt and equity. The shareholders contribute the equity portion of the company's capital. The debt portion may consist of loans from banks and financial institutions, money raised through bonds, fixed deposits, and secured or unsecured loans obtained from directors and other private parties. Shareholders, who are the owners of the company, have a right to the annual profits of the company after all its expenses have been met. As described earlier, part of these profits are ploughed back into the accumulated reserves of a company, while the remaining profits are distributed to its shareholders in the form of dividends. The net worth (also known as shareowners' funds) of a company comprises its equity plus its accumulated reserves. Therefore, the total capital employed by the company in its business operations comprises net worth plus debt.

Turning now to profits. The net profit of a company is the residual surplus it earns after meeting all expenses, including non-cash expenses such as depreciation on assets. The net profit is a useful figure, but it does not give us a true picture of a company's operating performance. To judge the operating performance we must look at a company's operating profit which is different from its net profit.

The figure for operating profit is arrived at after adding back taxes paid, depreciation, extraordinary one-time expenses, and deducting extraordinary one-time income and other income (income not earned through mainline operations), to the net profit figure. The operating profit of a company is a better indicator of the profits earned by it than is the net profit.

Return on capital employed

Return on capital employed (ROCE) is best defined as operating profit divided by capital employed (net worth plus debt).

ROCE thus reflects the overall earnings performance and operational efficiency of a company's business. It is an important basic ratio that permits an investor to make inter-company comparisons.

Return on net worth

Return on net worth (RONW) is defined as net profit divided by net worth. It is a basic ratio that tells a shareholder what he is getting out of his investment in the company.

ROCE is a better measure to get an idea of the overall profitability of the company's operations, while RONW is a better measure for judging the returns that a shareholder gets on his investment. The use of both these ratios will give a broad picture of a company's efficiency, financial viability and its ability to earn returns on shareholders' funds and capital employed.

PEG ratio

PEG is an important and widely used ratio for forming an estimate of the intrinsic value of a share. It tells you whether the share that you are interested in buying or selling is under-priced, fully priced or over-priced.

For this you need to link the P/E ratio to the future growth rate of the company. This is based on the assumption that the higher the expected growth rate of the company, the higher will be the P/E ratio that the company's share commands in the market. The reverse is equally true. The P/E ratio cannot be viewed in isolation. It has to be viewed in the context of the company's future growth rate. The PEG is calculated by dividing the P/E by the forecasted growth rate in the EPS (earnings per share) of the company.

As a broad rule of the thumb, a PEG value below 0.5 indicates a very attractive buying opportunity, whereas a selling opportunity emerges when the PEG crosses 1.5.

As a broad rule of the thumb, a PEG value below 0.5 indicates a very attractive buying opportunity, whereas a selling opportunity emerges when the PEG crosses 1.5, or even 2 for that matter. The catch here is to accurately calculate the future growth rate of earnings (EPS) of the company. Wide and intensive reading of investment and business news and analysis, combined with experience will certainly help you to make more accurate forecasts of company earnings.

CHAPTER 7

The right price and the right time

In chapters 4, 5 and 6 we dealt with the question: Which share to buy? The idea was to help you understand how to select suitable companies for investment. If you want to be a successful investor, however, you must not only know what to buy, but also when to buy it — and at what price to buy it. Further, in order to maximise your investment returns you must know when to sell a share, and what price to sell it at. The great fortunes on stock exchanges have been made not so much by those who knew what to buy and sell, but by those who mastered the art of buying and selling at the right time and price.

Using P/E ratio to assess share prices

The P/E ratio is one of the most important tools that an investor has for judging whether a particular share is over- or under-priced. Under-priced shares offer opportunities for buying, whereas over-priced shares offer opportunities for selling.

As a rule-of-thumb, avoid buying shares in companies which have a P/E ratio of more than 25

As a rule-of-thumb, avoid buying shares in companies which have a P/E ratio of more than 25 unless you are confident that your assessment of the company's future growth prospects justifies such a high P/E ratio. When you are buying shares in a large, well-known, growth-oriented company, you can't really go wrong if you buy its shares when its P/E ratio is around 15-20, or even lower. Such companies usually command

Table 7.1

Name of company: XYZ Ltd.

Year Ending		*31 Dec. 1999*	*31 Dec. 2000*	*31 Dec. 2001*
EPS (Rs. Per share)		3.0	3.5	4.5
Price (Rs. Per Share):	High	40	50	70
	Low	22	24	30
Average Price		31	37	50
$P/E = \frac{\text{Average Price}}{\text{EPS}}$		10.4	10.6	11.0

$$\text{Average P/E} = \frac{10.4 + 10.6 + 11.0}{3} = 10.7$$

Note:

(1) If you multiply the Average P/E by the EPS for 31 December 2001 (10.7 x 4.5) you will get a price of Rs. 48.15. The shares of XYZ Ltd. ought to be priced at around Rs. 48.15. This price is only a rough norm for helping you take investment decisions – it should not be applied rigidly.

(2) Information regarding EPS and High and Low prices for prominent companies is normally given in financial newspapers, business and investment magazines.

P/E ratios of around 15-20 and it won't be very often that you will get a chance to pick up their shares at a price which gives a P/E of 15. At that Point, the shares are bound to be under-priced and you are probably buying them during a temporary dip in prices. For super-growth shares, a P/E of over 25 would be justified but as a beginner it would be advisable to keep away from these. Many investors have burnt their fingers in the scramble to get rich fast through investments in super-growth shares. The prices of such shares are bound to be over-rated *vis-à-vis* in terms of their intrinsic worth and future growth possibilities, particularly during booms. You should also beware of investing in shares with a P/E ratio of 5 to 8, or even less. If a share has any investment value, it should normally not have such a low P/E. There is bound to be a catch in it, somewhere, which has probably escaped your notice. The market will not allow a good share to go at a price, which is low enough to give it a P/E less than 5, unless it knows that the future of the company is uncertain and clouded.

A company's P/E does not normally deviate much from its average value over a period of around 3 to 5 years. Therefore, if you calculate the average P/E for a particular company for the previous 3 to 5 years, you can use it as a frame of reference for judging what the price of the company's shares ought to be under average conditions. How this can be done is illustrated in Table 7.1.

How book value may be useful

As we saw in the previous chapter, book value per share has only a limited utility for assessing share prices. However, within the limitations that were pointed out, and under certain conditions, it can be used as a rough norm for judging share prices.

In newly established companies, for instance, there should not be much of a variation between the market price of a share and its book value. For such companies, book value per share is a more reliable indicator for judging whether the company's shares are over-priced or under-priced.

In older companies, on the other hand, the gap between the market price of a share and its book value usually increases. For such companies, book value per share ceases to be of much use for evaluating what the price of its shares ought to be. However, even for such companies you should beware of buying a share whose market price is more than say, triple or quadruple its book value because at such levels, in all likelihood, it is over-priced. On the other hand, if the market price of an established company's share is around the same as its book value, the chances are that the share is under-priced.

Using the previous year's "highs" and "lows"

The highest and lowest prices recorded by a particular share in the previous year are helpful in providing a frame of reference for judging its current prices. If the price of a share is higher than its last year's peak price, then in all likelihood the share is either fully priced or over-priced. In fact, it may even be at its new peak price. On the other hand, if you pick up a sound growth share at around its previous year's lowest price, or even at the previous year's average price, then chances are that you are buying it at the right price. If the market price of a share far outstrips its previous year's peak price, it can be interpreted as a signal for selling that share. This is how the "highs" and "lows" of the past year can be used for evaluation of current share prices. The basic rule to remember is that in a growing economy, the current year's highs and lows of a share will usually be higher than its previous year's highest and lowest prices.

Making the most of booms and recessions

Booms and recessions are cyclical phenomena. No boom lasts forever. Sooner or later it inevitably gives way to a recession. A boom means that the economy has over-extended itself and a correction in the form of recession becomes due in order to restore its balance. Similarly, no recession lasts forever. It has, inevitably, to give way to improved conditions that again lead to a boom.

As a general rule, therefore, don't buy shares during a boom.

During a boom, share markets soar and there is a steep and widespread rise in share prices. Most shares thus get grossly over-priced, many even rise to unprecedented levels. As a general rule, therefore, don't buy shares during a boom. A boom is the time to sell shares, not for buying them. During a boom most share prices hit their peak levels and if you don't sell at the peak, when will you!

Conversely, a recession is the opportune time for buying shares at cheap prices. During a recession share markets over-react with a general, all-round fall in share prices to unjustifiably low levels. At such times most shares are grossly under-priced, so almost any share you buy will give you an excellent return on your investment once the economy pulls out of the recession. Therefore, as a general rule, do not miss out on the opportunity for making a large part of your investments during a recession.

Do not miss out on the opportunity for making a large part of your investments during a recession.

All of this sounds very simple to follow but what actually happens is that most investors end up doing the very opposite; they actually buy during a boom and sell during a recession! During a boom, a heady feeling of optimism and cheer permeates the economy and most people tend to view the future through rose-tinted glasses, confident that the good time will last forever. As a result, instead of selling shares they go in for heavy buying in the hope of making still bigger profits. Many investors even borrow money at high rates of interest for financing their investments. This is exactly what happened during the stock market boom in March-April 1992 which was fuelled by bank-siphoned funds. Similarly, during a recession when an atmosphere of gloom and pessimism pervades the economy, most people are hesitant to buy shares because they fear that share prices may fall still further. At such times, there is a scramble to sell everything at whatever the going price is, in a desperate bid to pull out in the fear that the market would forever go on falling. This just shows how easily people get influenced by their environment into taking irrational and untimely investment decisions.

Four simple rules for selling

Sound selling decisions are often more difficult to take than buying decisions. Here are four simple rules which should help you in this regard.

Rule 1: Don't wait for the "highest price"

Most investors wait for share prices to peak before selling. This may seem to be the obvious way to get the best price for your shares but the difficulty lies in judging when a particular share has actually reached its peak. Since share prices have a tendency to fall steeply — and suddenly — after touching the peak, the chances are that you may end up selling at a much lower price than what you had intended. Therefore, don't wait for share prices to peak before selling — sell as soon as you feel that you have made adequate profits on your investment. Buying low and selling high does not necessarily imply that you must buy at the lowest dip and sell at the highest peak. Therefore, don't allow yourself to get obsessed with the idea that in order to make money on the stock markets you must only buy at the lowest dip and sell at the highest peak. Most successful investors make a lot of money — and get excellent returns on their share investments — by buying and selling in an intermediate range of prices.

Rule 2: Sell a share when your target price is reached

When you buy shares of a particular company, you do so with a certain goal in mind.

For example, you may have bought them with the intention of doubling your investment in two years. We recommend that you sell the shares the moment you reach, or cross, your target. If your shares double in less than two years, you should sell them straightaway because you have already achieved your objective and there is no point in holding on any longer. If prices continue to rise after you have sold the shares you may feel that you have missed out on the opportunity of making more money. While this may be true you should also keep in mind the converse possibility; that the price may fall after you have sold your shares. In that case it will result in your failing to achieve your investment objective. In the long run, you will make more money if you consistently and regularly achieve your investment goals, than by trying to over-achieve by squeezing additional gains from each transaction.

Rule 3: Once you realise you may have made a mistake – sell!

You buy a share on the basis of a careful assessment of the future working of a company. It may nevertheless turn out to be a bad investment. In such a situation we recommend that you sell your shares immediately, even if it means incurring a substantial loss. There is no point in holding on in the vague hope that things may eventually improve; wishful thinking is not the way to get rich in the stock markets. If some investment turns out to be bad, admit your mistake, cut your losses, and pull out without further delay. Remember, you are not alone in making mistakes. Even the most successful stock market operators, the ones who have amassed millions, readily admit that they too frequently make mistakes. Despite that they have succeeded in making a lot of money. So will you, provided you understand the importance of cutting your losses.

Rule 4: Sell a share if you wouldn't buy it at its prevailing price

How to decide which share to sell and which to keep. Every investor has to make this decision ever so often. A shrewd and foresighted investor sells regularly, not only for encashing capital gains but also for improving his portfolio by adding shares of companies belonging to newly emerging high-growth sectors of the economy. We suggest a simple rule for deciding which share to sell and which to keep: "Don't hold a share which you wouldn't buy."

In most cases you will find this a useful rule-of-the thumb technique for updating your portfolio. The reasons for holding on to a share are virtually the same as those for buying it. If you are not prepared to buy a share at a particular market price, then there is no reason why you should keep it. There is no point in holding on to a share simply because you already possess it. So always ask yourself the question. "Is this share worth buying at its present price?" If not, then you should sell it immediately because if a share is not worth buying at its current price, then it is not worth holding on to either!

Some suggestions for better timing

There are no hard and fast rules about the proper timing of investment decision. The art of buying and selling shares at the right time cannot really be reduced to any formula — it can be picked up only through personal experience. However, we give below some suggestions, which should be useful in deciding when to buy and sell:

1. Don't buy a share immediately after a steep rise in its price. A steep rise is usually followed by a steep fall; the steeper the rise, the greater the subsequent fall. When share prices fall, they usually retrace about one-third to two-thirds of the price range covered by the earlier rise. Thus, if the price of a share rises from Rs. 40 to 55, then in the subsequent fall its price will probably drop to about Rs. 45 to Rs 50 per share. And that is the appropriate time for buying it, i.e. after its price has fallen in reaction to the earlier rise.

2. If you want to sell a share, do so immediately after a steep rise in its price. The chances are that you will then be selling at around one of its peaks, which it may not touch again for quite some time.

3. Don't sell a share immediately after a steep fall in its prices. Chances are that the share prices will rally by recovering around one-third to two-third of the lost ground. The appropriate time to sell it would be during the ensuing rally when you can get a better price.

4. A sharp fall in prices offers an opportunity for buying, provided you are confident that the fall in prices is purely temporary and that the future outlook of the company is promising enough to ensure that the subsequent rise in price will go far beyond the level from which it earlier fell.

5. If you have a promising growth share in mind the best time to buy it is when the public loses interest in the share and when a considerable period of time has passed since it was last in the news. If you buy a share at a time when it is basking in the full glare of publicity, then the chances are that you will be picking it up at, or around, one of its peak prices. Try to pick up a share in anticipation of good news rather than after the good news has become widely known. Conversely, the best time to sell is either after some widely publicised good news, or when the share is the centre of favourable public attention.

6. Share prices usually record a sharp rise just before any expansion project of a company becomes operational. If you are a buyer, than you should do your buying around a month or so before this happens. On the other hand, if you are a seller you should sell a couple of months after the plant goes into commercial production so that you can take full advantage of that price rise.

7. Companies often issue press releases about their expansion plans, diversification plans, plans to issue better-selling new products, rising order book position and proposals to issue bonus shares, rights shares, rights convertible debentures, etc. News of this nature has a bullish effect on share prices. Therefore if you want to buy shares in such a company, do not delay placing a buy order with your broker. Ideally, it would be best if you bought the shares on the same day the news item first appears in newspapers. The same rule should be followed when companies release their half-yearly working results to the press, indicating improved performance.

CHAPTER 8

Investing in public issues (IPOs)

There are basically two ways in which you can buy shares: you can either buy them from the stock market (as described in Chapter 3), or you can apply for them in a public issue. The stock market is a secondary market where shares are bought and sold, whereas the primary market is one where companies issue shares for the first time. This chapter deals with the primary market where IPOs (initial public offerings) are issued to investors.

When a company raises funds by issuing new shares or debentures for sale to the public, it is called a public issue, or an IPO (initial public offering). Such new shares and debentures are called new issues. New issues of capital can be made by existing companies as well as by new companies. Bonus shares and rights shares are also new issues but since they are only issued to existing shareholders of the company, they are not called public issues.

How profitable are public issues?

Public issues provide you with an opportunity for picking up shares at relatively low prices. Newly formed companies usually offer their shares for subscription at par values, whereas existing companies price their new issues at levels which are sometimes as much as 20 to 30 per cent lower than the market price of their existing shares. For example, new issues priced at Rs. 12 to Rs 15 per share may be quoted as high as Rs. 20 to Rs. 25 per share in the secondary market soon after their listing on the bourses.

Similarly, shares issued at par by new companies also quote at high premiums soon after they get listed on the stock exchange. For example, in early 2004 public issues of Maruti Udyog, Indraprastha Gas and Divi's Labs listed at high premiums.

This is the main reason why public issues are so popular with investors; they offer opportunities for making quick money which few other forms of investment can hope to match. The only snag lies in getting a firm allotment of shares. Since most good public issues are heavily oversubscribed, lots have to be drawn and only a few of the applicants succeed in getting a firm allotment. Sometimes the allotment is done on a proportionate basis. Therefore, you should consider yourself lucky if you get an allotment of even a small number of shares. It is with this background in mind that you should calculate the pros and cons of applying for IPOs.

Applying for an IPO

IPOs are generally given widespread, nation-wide publicity through advertisements in newspapers and magazines well before the date fixed for the opening of their issues. These advertisements, along with the other highlights of the issue, give the names and addresses of brokers and the bankers to the issue from whom you can get copies of the prospectus and application forms. If you write to any one of them, they will send you the prospectus and application forms free of cost.

The prospectus is a document inviting the public to purchase or subscribe to the shares of the company. It contains all relevant information you may need to decide whether a company is worth investing in. It would, therefore, be in your interest to read a company's prospectus carefully before applying for its shares.

The subscription list is required to be kept open for a minimum of three days and a maximum of ten days. Since most of the IPOs are oversubscribed, the subscription list is usually closed immediately after three to five days. You have to submit your application form and the stipulated application money to any one of the banks or their branches listed on the reverse of the application form. Applications, whether handed personally or sent by post, should reach the bank within the period during which the subscription list remains open.

If you are lucky and get an allotment, the company will send you an allotment letter which will inform you that shares allotted to you have been credited to your demat account. Nowadays, for IPOs with an issue size of Rs. 10 crore or more, shares are issued only in the demat form. For IPOs with an issue size of Rs. 100 crore or more, shares are issued only through the book building process.

Where the IPO is issued through the book building process, reservations are made for QIBs (qualified institutional buyers), non-institutional buyers (large investors), and retail investors who apply for less than Rs. 50,000 worth of shares. What exactly is book building? Book building is a process whereby the demand for a share is ascertained so that it can be issued at the maximum price. Before the opening of the public issue, the lead manager to the issue announces a price band in which the company plans to allot the shares. For example, in the case ONGC's public issue in March 2004 the price band was Rs. 680 to Rs. 750 per share. After the issue, the cut-off price is fixed in such a manner that all the shares are offloaded to the QIBs and the public either at, or above, the cut-off price. In this way the company gets the maximum price for its shares.

Companies cannot allot shares arbitrarily. They do so in consultation with the stock exchange authorities. The principles on which allotment is done are heavily weighted in favour of large applicants.

If you are living in a city where one or more bank branches have been designated for accepting application forms, you should give in your application only on the third, or closing, day of the subscription list. On the first two days you should visit the concerned banks for making an on-the-spot assessment of the public response to the issue. If the public response is poor, then your chances of getting a firm allotment are brighter. On the other hand, if the public response is very heavy, then your chances of getting an allotment will obviously be very poor and it may not be worthwhile to apply at all. The enthusiasm with which the public responds to a particular issue will also give you an idea of the premium the shares are likely to subsequently command after listing. The greater the public interest in any share, the higher will be the price at which it is later likely to be quoted in the stock markets.

The gap between the issue price of a share and the price at which it is initially quoted on the stock exchange is in the nature of a windfall gain.

The gap between the issue price of a share and the price at which it is initially quoted on the stock exchange is in the nature of a windfall gain. Should you get a firm allotment in any issue, don't miss out on the opportunity to encash these gains unless you want to retain the share as a long-term investment for tax purposes. If you sell a share at a premium soon after it is allotted to you, your money is freed for recycling in other new issues and you can maximise the returns on your investments in public issues.

Some guidelines for investing in new issues

New issues can be divided into two broad groups:

- New issues of newly formed companies, and
- New issues of existing companies.

New issues of existing companies are, by and large, very good investments. They provide an opportunity for acquiring shares in ongoing profit-making companies at relatively low prices. On the other hand, all new issues of newly formed companies are not good investments. You have to be careful in selecting a new company to invest in, as the incidence of failure among these is quite high. We give below some guidelines which should help you select the right new issues for investment:

1. Don't invest blindly in a company having unknown and untried promoters. First study the performance of other companies set up by the same promoters. If these have done well, then chances of the new one doing well are also high.

2. Don't invest in a company which is not ready to start business operations. This will help you avoid investing in companies which may have long gestation periods before business operation can commence.

3. Invest in companies that have something new to offer. Companies introducing a new product or industrial process for the first time, companies proposing to manufacture a product which is currently being imported, companies introducing a technologically advanced or better quality product, or companies venturing into new areas are likely to be better and more remunerative investments.

4. Invest in companies that operate in high-growth sectors of the economy. The incidence of failure is likely to be lower for such companies.

5. Avoid investing in very small companies. This point has been discussed earlier in Chapter 5.

6. Check the reputation and market standing of the foreign collaborator, if there is one. For example, new issues of Vesuvius India and Birla Ericsson evoked a very good response from investors because of the excellent international reputation of their parent companies.

7. Companies where the foreign collaborator has an equity stake are often good investments. Foreign collaborators do not readily opt for an equity stake in any company unless they are confident of its bright future prospects.

8. Do apply for the mega issues of well-known profit-earning companies. The sheer size of such issues ensures better chances of getting a firm allotment. This is what happened in the public issue of the State Bank of India. The bigger the size of the issue, the better will be your chances of getting a firm allotment.

CHAPTER 9

How to identify profitable investment opportunities

Though investment opportunities abound all the time and in almost all situations, often they may not be very easy to identify. A shrewd and discerning investor will usually find opportunities for making money in places, and in situations, where a less discerning one will not. The best investment opportunities are often found in the most unlikely places and situations. For example, in the beginning of 1994 few could have predicted that the shares of the then relatively unknown company like Infosys Technologies, focusing primarily on Y2K software projects, would provide one of the best investment opportunities of the last decade.

In this chapter we shall identify and discuss some typical situations which provide excellent investment opportunities.

Turnaround situations

A turnaround situation exists when a company that has been making losses for a number of years starts turning the corner and is expected to begin making profits. Since the company has been making losses, its shares are likely to be quoted at very low prices, often below par. Once the company wipes out its accumulated losses and begins to make profits, its changed fortunes are bound to be reflected in a sharp and steep rise in the price of its shares. This rise can be as high as 200 to 300 per cent in one year.

SAIL (Steel Authority of India) is an outstanding example of a successful turnaround company in recent years. At one stage, in October 2003, its share price had fallen to as low a figure as Rs 6 per share. Due to a turnaround in the fortunes of the steel industry and the company by early 2004, its share price had soared to Rs 55 per share, notching up a capital appreciation of 916 per cent in a matter of a little over three months.

However, while investing in a turnaround company you should make sure that the reversal in the company's performance is not going to be a flash in the pan and short-lived. The turnaround should be sustained over a sufficiently long period of time for an investor to make profits from it. It often happens that the performance of a company initially shows signs of a promising recovery but nosedives soon after. You have, therefore, to be careful in picking up potential turnaround companies.

Amalgamations and mergers

The amalgamation of one company with another, or the merger of two companies into one company, is normally advantageous for both companies. Amalgamations and mergers are mostly resorted to with the object of strengthening the finances and operations of both companies by forming one consolidated company. In some cases of amalgamations or mergers, a high growth, profit-making company combines with a company which has large accumulated losses so that substantial tax benefits can be derived by setting off the profits of the former against the losses of the latter. Sometimes, companies manufacturing similar or complementary products and catering to overlapping markets find it advantageous to merge because they can substantially cut down on overhead, and operational and sales expenses. Similarly, overhead and other expenses can be trimmed considerably if a company merges with its own subsidiary company. It is also much easier for a company to diversify and grow by merging with an established company than by setting up new units and nursing them through their gestation periods.

After the merger, the new combined company generally performs much better than the combined performance of its component companies prior to the merger. Hence, news of impending amalgamations and mergers always has a bullish effect on share prices of the companies involved. This is the main reason why companies going in for amalgamations and mergers provide an attractive investment opportunity. A prominent example of a recent merger in India was that of ASEA with Hindustan Brown Boveri to form ABB Ltd. Earlier, the four ICI companies — Crescent Dyes, Chemicals & Fibres, Alkali & Chemicals and Indian Explosives had merged into one giant conglomerate known as IEL, which has now been named ICI India Ltd.

Takeovers and acquisitions

A takeover is initiated when a business house, a company, or a group of companies acting in concert take over a large enough chunk of another company's shares to displace the old management and give the new management complete control over the company. A takeover bid usually results in frantic, large-scale buying of shares by both the competing groups in an effort to acquire more shares than the other. As a result, share prices are pushed up to levels far above their intrinsic worth.

Takeover bids, whether successful or not, provide an opportunity for ordinary investors to make money. In addition, takeovers often benefit the company and its shareholders by giving it a new, dynamic and growth-oriented management. Often this factor alone provides a good reason for investing in the shares of a company which is the target of a takeover bid. In 1983, alleged takeover bids pushed up the share prices of Escorts from Rs. 40 to Rs. 80 per share, of DCM from Rs. 35 to Rs. 105 per share, and of Textool from Rs. 120 to Rs. 435 per share.

Sometimes a company, a business house or a group of companies acting in concert acquire control over another company through a negotiated purchase of the shareholding of the existing management. This is different from the usual takeover bid because it doesn't involve large-scale competitive buying of shares in the stock markets and, therefore, doesn't really have a big impact on the company's share prices. In such cases, share prices usually move up or down depending upon the reputation and record of the company's new management. One example is the acquisition by the Hinduja-Iveco combine of the controlling interest in Ashok Leyland. As a result, the shares of Ashok Leyland rose from a low of around Rs. 30 per share in 1987 to as high as Rs. 86 per share in April 1989. Other prominent examples of recent takeovers and acquisitions have been the abortive Ambani takeover of Larsen & Turbo, the successful takeover of BSES by Reliance, the Chhabria takeover of Hindustan Dorr Oliver, the Mallya takeover of Best and Crompton, and the Tata takeover of ACC.

Changes in government policies

Major changes in government policies often benefit some companies by opening up new avenues for growth and higher profits and such companies provide excellent investment opportunities for investors who are quick in recognising the implications of such policy changes. In the early 1980s, removal of price controls over cement ushered in a period of high growth for ACC and other cement companies. In 1988, the lifting of price controls over aluminium boosted the profits of companies, like Hindustan Aluminium and Indian Aluminium. Later, the strong package of financial incentives and disincentives contained in the budgets for 1993-94 and 1994-95 ushered in a period of high growth for computer software companies, like Infosys Technologies, Wipro, Satyam Computers, I-flex and Rolta; hotel companies, such as

Indian Hotels, East India Hotels and Asian Hotel, and power sector companies, like Tata Power and BSES (now called Reliance Energy).

Changes in government policy can also sometimes affect a company adversely. If you are a shareholder and are quick to foresee the implication of such a change, you can sell your shares before their prices begin to fall. For example, the cuts in customs duties on imported steel items in 2004 made it more difficult for Indian steel companies, like SAIL, TISCO and Essar Gujarat to compete with cheap steel imports. Shrewd investors reacted quickly to these disadvantageous budgetary provisions and immediately offloaded their steel shares. However, these detrimental changes in excise and customs duties did not necessarily imply the death-knell of the steel industry. The long-term prospects of well-managed steel companies continue to be bright, notwithstanding the inevitable erosion of their profits in the short run due to increased competition from cheaper imports.

Technological innovations

We are living in a society which is being increasingly dominated by technology. Accordingly, alert investors on the lookout for big gains will find suitable investment opportunities in companies, which go in for technological innovations in a big way. For example, IT services companies, bio-technology companies and telecommunication companies are major beneficiaries of technological changes.

Anticipating the future

The best investment opportunities are available to those who can successfully anticipate the future. If you can identify the future areas or directions of growth, you would have identified when and where to invest for maximum returns. Making an accurate assessment of future conditions and future growth areas is not as easy as it sounds — it involves a lot of study and analysis. If you want to be a successful investor, such study and analysis are very necessary. Investment is an activity which by its very nature involves looking into the future. Unless you look into the future and form a personal viewpoint on what it will be like, you will not be able to decide where and when to invest your money. For an investor, anticipating the future is unavoidable.

How do you anticipate the future? The best way to do so is to be always alert to what is happening around you. The seeds of the future are present today.

For example, if you live in an industrial city or area, you cannot help but notice the steadily deteriorating condition of the environment. Water and air are becoming rapidly polluted. The day is not far off when the pollution levels will become intolerable and will pose a major health hazard to the population. Environmental pollution is becoming an area of serious concern to the public and the government. The Water Pollution and Air Pollution Acts have already been passed by Parliament and the government has established a new department, known as the Department of Environment, for implementing these laws. All these developments are pointers to an emerging high-growth area, namely, the manufacture of air pollution and water pollution control equipment. These developments also point to a high growth in healthcare.

International trends

Globalisation is the buzzword since the 1990s. No country in the world can now hope to remain immune from the influence of international economic trends. As a result, it has now become imperative for Indian stock market investors to keep a close watch on international economic developments and to analyse their likely impact on the performance of Indian companies. For example, the signing of the WTO (World Trade Organisation) agreement has opened up high growth opportunities for Indian food, pharma, textile and IT exporters.

It has also created the conditions required for a sustained long-term growth in the volume of world sea-borne trade, thus significantly improving the prospects of Indian shipping companies, like Great Eastern Shipping and Shipping Corporation of India.

In the 21st century, a stock market investor who is aware of what is happening in the larger world beyond India's borders and who keeps a close tab on major international developments will definitely find himself in a more advantageous position *vis-a-vis* an inward-looking investor whose awareness is confined only to what happens within the country.

Sunrise industries

The term sunrise industries refers to the new and emerging industries of the future. Early investment made in those companies which have been correctly identified as the future leaders of such nascent industries have always provided and will continue to provide truly attractive returns to patient and farsighted investors.

In the 1960s, for example, the sunrise industries in India were scooters, synthetic textiles, and five-star hotel chains. If at that time you had bought shares in Bajaj Auto, Indian Hotels, Century Spinning (now known as Century Textiles) or Gwalior Rayon (now renamed Grasim) you could have accumulated a huge fortune in the last 30 years.

The sunrise industries of the 21st century are likely to be computer software, computer training, bio-technology, electronic mail, processed foods, telecommunications, corporate hospitals, budget hotels, private airlines, oil exploration, pollution control, diagnostic kits, fast-food chains and departmental stores. If you are serious about making money then you simply cannot afford to ignore these industries. We suggest that you allocate at least one-third of your portfolio to the more promising companies operating in these sunrise industries.

CHAPTER 10

Know yourself and your fellow investors

In this chapter we review certain aspects of individual and market behaviour that are commonly observed in the stock markets. This will help you understand how and why people act in the manner that they do when they enter into stock market transactions. This knowledge will help you to understand not only your own behaviour but also give you a deeper insight into the causes and motivations behind the behaviour of your fellow investors. An understanding of how people behave in the stock markets will enable you to make more money through better and wiser investment decisions.

Human beings are basically irrational

Most human beings act irrationally most of the time. They are motivated by all kinds of emotions, impulses of the moment, instincts, prejudices, wishful thinking, hopes, fears, desires — almost everything, except logic and reason. These motives influence the buying and selling decisions of investors and other stock market operators in the same way that they influence their decisions in other spheres of human activity. Therefore, you should not try to understand stock market behaviour solely on the basis of intelligence, reason and logic. If you do so, you are likely to make serious errors in your investment calculations and decisions.

If human beings were to always behave rationally and logically then both stock prices and their future movements would be totally predictable. Share prices, in such a situation, would generally hover closely around their intrinsic values and opportunities for making money by buying under-priced shares and selling them when they become over-priced would virtually disappear. The fact that this does not happen is ample evidence that human beings do not act rationally and logically all the time.

We are all part of a crowd

A crowd is a collection of people gathered in one place. Stock market investors and speculators may not be present in one place physically but mentally they are all linked together in the same way as is an actual crowd. They read the same newspapers, they deal with the same group of stockbrokers, they watch the same share price movements, and they tend to react to news and events in the same manner. For all practical purposes, therefore, the market is a crowd, and stock market behaviour can best be understood and interpreted if viewed as crowd behaviour.

Crowd behaviour is very different from the behaviour of individuals who make up the crowd. A crowd never reasons or thinks — it is always swayed by emotions. Emotions being extremely contagious sweep through the crowd — sometimes propelling it in one direction, at other times in another. This is the reason why crowds are never moderate in their approach — they are always given to extremes of behaviour. They also over-react, pushing share prices up to unrealistically high levels or stamping them down to very low levels. Over-reaction is a universal phenomenon exhibited by stock markets all over the world. Shrewd and knowledgeable investors make money by taking advantage of the fact that share prices always over-react — they pick up grossly under-priced shares and sell them when they become grossly over-priced.

In order to do so, however, you should be able to insulate yourself from the contagion of the crowd. Don't be drawn into the crowd — stay outside it. This is easier said than done, of course. But if you wish to be a successful investor you will have to learn to keep your head when everyone else seems to be losing theirs. Study crowd behaviour, watch the crowd in action, anticipate and predict its movements but don't become a part of it. People belonging to the crowd never make much money; they only provide an opportunity for others to do so.

Admit your mistakes

Most human beings find it very difficult to admit their mistakes. They usually rationalise and invent reasons for justifying their actions and assessments, put the blame on somebody else, ascribe their misfortunes to ill-luck or fate — in fact, do everything but admit that they have been wrong. Failure to admit one's mistakes can be disastrous in the stock markets.

Unless you admit your mistakes, you will not know when and where to cut your losses. There is nothing unusual about making a mistake. Everybody makes mistakes, particularly when buying and selling shares. Even the most successful stock market operators readily admit that they make mistakes quite frequently. There is an oft-quoted stock market maxim: "Every time a share is bought or sold, somebody somewhere has made a mistake." Therefore, don't be ashamed to admit your mistakes. The quicker you are in admitting your mistakes, the easier you will find it to pull out of bad investments in time.

Greed and fear

Greed and fear are the two most dominant emotions found in the stock markets. They are the two extreme aspects of crowd behaviour. Greed is the most prevalent emotion in a rising market; fear takes over in a falling one. Greed causes frantic buying whereas fear causes panic selling. It is because of greed and fear that the markets always over-react in booms and depressions. If it were not for greed and fear, share prices would not fluctuate as violently and as erratically as they actually do.

Whenever you find that you have achieved or crossed your investment objectives, you should sell. Don't be greedy and hold on to your shares in the expectation of further gains. An overbought market is highly unstable and may collapse at any moment. On the other hand, don't panic into selling after a steep fall in share prices. Remember, that recessions and slumps are temporary phenomena — sooner or later they are bound to give way to a rising market. If you hold on, you will find that the subsequent rise in prices is likely to compensate you amply for the waiting period.

Don't be a snob

Snobbery is as prevalent in the stock markets as in other areas of life. There are many investors who buy shares not because of their intrinsic worth, but because of their snob value. Even their investment selections are dictated by the snob value of various scrips. Shares of companies having impressive, foreign-sounding names and marketing products with prestigious brand names and clientele are preferred for investment as compared to companies belonging to newly formed Indian business houses. Avoid being a snob. Snobbery doesn't pay in the stock market. Foreign sounding names are not necessarily gateways to wealth and riches. You will do well to base your investment decisions on things more solid and realistic than mere snobbery!

Seeing the reality for what it is

Many of us view the stock market with preconceived notions and ideas. We think that the market actually is what we think it ought to be. Most of us make the mistake of substituting reality with wishful thinking. The market is not concerned with what you think it ought to be. It is what it is. If you wish to be successful, you will have to learn to view it as it is, and not as what you would have it to be.

Don't get influenced by your own concept of an ideal market while making your buying and selling decisions. Don't let preconceptions and wishful thinking influence you — be objective and realistic in your approach to investment matters.

Keeping up with your neighbours

Many people buy shares in a particular company simply because all their friends and colleagues seem to have shares in it. They do so because they don't want to be left out. Don't buy shares in a company simply to keep up with the Joneses. There is no reason to presume that your neighbours and colleagues have better investment knowledge and judgement than you. In fact, keeping up with the Joneses is one of the ways in which you get sucked into the crowd. As we have seen earlier, being part of a crowd is not likely to get you anywhere. You must always retain your objectivity and independence of judgement while taking investment decisions.

Learn to take risks

When you decide to buy shares you are knowingly and willingly exposing yourself to a variety of risks. The shares you buy may not appreciate in value or, worse, their price may actually plummet, leaving you with a capital loss. The company whose shares you buy may not perform as well as you expect, or even if its performance were to live up to your most optimistic expectations the market may not be sufficiently enthused over it to push up its share price. Moral: don't buy shares unless

Moral: don't buy shares unless you are emotionally and temperamentally prepared to take some risks.

you are emotionally and temperamentally prepared to take some risks.

Once you decide to enter the stock market, then don't let the possibility of making losses prevent you from taking reasonable and calculated risks. The higher the risk, the greater the potential rewards. Low risks invariably imply low returns. Therefore, don't play safe. Learn to take risks. If you don't risk your capital, you will be depriving yourself of the only realistic chance you will ever have of becoming rich. Remember, the economic structure of the world is rigged in favour of the bold risk-taker.

How do you know that you are taking sufficient risks? The first sign after you have made a risky investment will be a feeling of unease and anxiety. If any investment gives you a feeling of smug satisfaction, then it means that you have not taken the required degree of risk necessary to earn big profits. The best investments are those that make you toss and turn in your bed at night and not those that give you sound, carefree sleep. Remember, as an investor your main goal is making money and not sound sleep. As the Swiss say, a "state of worry" is the price you pay for the opportunity of making money.

CHAPTER 11

A step-by-step guide to actual investing

By now you must be keen to get down to making your first investment in shares. In order to help you do so, we give below a simple step-by-step summary procedure for selecting the right share to invest in.

Preliminary screening

Don't buy unlisted shares.

Don't buy inactive shares.
An inactive share is one which is transacted less than twice a month.

Don't buy shares in a closely held company.
A closely held company in India would be one which has less than 10,000 shareholders.

Examining the company

What is the quality of the company's management?
Is it dynamic, growth-oriented and forward-looking? Is the management free from factionalism and in-fighting?

How large is the company?

Avoid investing in a company with an equity capital of less than Rs. 10 crore and sales less than Rs. 100 crore.

Does the company concentrate on its core competence or is it sufficiently diversified?

Avoid investing in a one-product, one-plant, one-market company that is not an industry leader in its field or in a company that has overly diversified into unrelated businesses.

Is it a growth company?

What are the company's future plans for expansion-cum-diversification? Avoid investing in a company that is not growth-oriented, or one which has no concrete plans for growth.

What is the company's environment like?

Is the company's environment conducive to growth or not? Avoid investing in a company functioning in an adverse or hostile environment.

Does the company have labour problems?

Avoid investing in a company which has chronic and seemingly never-ending labour problems.

Analysing the company's finances

Ploughback

Is the company retaining a sufficient portion of its profits as ploughback? Growth companies normally retain two-thirds or more of their profits as ploughback.

Reserves

What is the size of the company's reserves compared to its equity capital? High reserves, more than double the equity capital, indicate the possibility of your receiving a liberal bonus issue.

Book value per share

Calculate the company's book value per share. How does it compare with the market price of the company's shares? The closer the market price of a share is to its book value, the greater the possibility of the share being under-priced.

Earnings per share (EPS)

Calculate the company's EPS. It will give you an idea of what each share earns. This will help you evaluate the market price of the share.

Price/Earning (P/E) ratio

Calculate the company's P/E ratio. This will give you an idea of how long it will take you to recover your investment in the company's shares at the prevailing market prices. Avoid investing in companies with a P/E of more than 10.

Yield

Calculate the company's yield. It will give an idea of what you can expect by way of regular income, if you buy the company's shares at the present market price. Average yield figures usually hover around 2 per cent of the market value of the shares. Growth shares generally have lower yields

ROCE, RONW and PEG ratios

These will enable you to get a fix on what the company ought to be worth, and how efficiently it is using its capital.

The above information for Indian companies is readily available in financial magazines and investment websites listed in Appendix A.

Making an investment decision

The decision to buy has three parts to it:

1. What to buy?
2. At what price to buy it? and
3. When to buy?

What to buy?

After carefully assessing the information gathered on the various points listed above, you should prepare a short list of companies that appear to be the best investment.

At what price to buy it?

Use the company's P/E ratio, PEG ratio, book value per share, and the previous year's "high" and "low" prices to calculate what the price of the company's shares ought to be. Discard those companies whose shares appear to be clearly over-priced.

When to buy?

Use the various hints and techniques listed in Chapter 7 for the proper timing of your buying decisions.

CHAPTER 12

Investing in mutual funds

No book on investment nowadays can afford to ignore mutual funds. In fact, since 1993 most new Indian individual investors have got their first taste of stock market only through mutual funds. Though mutual funds have been the most popular form of investment in USA and other developed free-market countries for the last two decades, the average Indian investor was first exposed to them in a big way only in 1986. At present there are over 200 mutual funds schemes in India compared to over 3,000 such registered funds in USA alone. At a rough estimate, a vast majority of the 50 million investors in India have already invested in these funds and the number is growing every year. Though relatively new on the Indian stock market scene, with their pooled resources of over Rs.1,50,000 crore, mutual funds exercise a major influence on share price movements in the Indian stock markets.

What are mutual funds?

There is no universally accepted or legal definition of the term mutual fund. It is a loose term which embraces a wide variety of investment companies. Broadly speaking, a mutual fund is an investment company that invests — generally in stock market securities — the pooled funds of its shareholders. In UK such companies are known as investment trusts whereas in USA they are commonly referred to as mutual funds.

Thus, a mutual fund invests the money it collects from its unit holders on their behalf. For instance, when you invest in an equity fund, you don't directly buy shares from the stock market; the mutual fund does so on your behalf. Accordingly, equity funds offer you another method of investing in shares instead of directly buying and selling them from the stock market. It is the fund manager who decides which shares to buy, and when to buy and sell them.

Making money from mutual funds

A mutual fund earns money from two sources:

1. Dividends or interest from its investments in shares and bonds, and
2. Capital gains on sale of investments that have appreciated in price minus the capital losses on sales of investments that have depreciated in price.

A mutual fund either distributes its profits (less fees and expenses) in part or in full to its unit holders, or ploughs them back into the fund for further appreciation of its NAV. The unit holders get returns through capital appreciation arising from an increase in the NAV of the fund and through the dividends that the fund declares. There is currently a very wide choice available for selecting the right kind of mutual fund that suits your requirements.

Types of mutual funds

While there is now a wide variety of mutual fund schemes available to the Indian investor, in this book we will briefly review essentially the different types of equity funds since only such funds invest your money in shares.

Equity funds

Equity funds, also known as growth-oriented funds, provide mainly capital appreciation for their unit holders. The growth, or capital appreciation, comes from the fact that such funds invest almost their entire corpus exclusively in equities. If you want high returns from these funds, then your timing for entry and exit becomes crucial for success. Equity funds give very high returns only if you invest in them during a bear market bottom, or a level that is close to the bottom. Investments made in these funds during a bull market top, or a level that is close to the top, will probably give you negative returns. This is also the reason why the NAVs of equity funds are more volatile than those of the other types of funds. However, the overall experience is that over the long term, return from equity funds tend to outperform returns from investments in other types of funds.

Index funds

Index funds are funds whose investments mirror a selected market index, such as the BSE Sensitive Index (Sensex), S&P NSE 50 Index (Nifty), etc. These schemes invest in all the shares included in the selected index, giving the same weightage to different shares in the composition of their portfolio as the weightage given to them in the index. As a result the performance of an index fund closely resembles the performance of the index. These funds generally have a good track record since worldwide experience has shown that most funds, in the long run, are unable to outperform even the indices.

Sector funds

As their name suggests, these are funds which invest in shares of companies belonging to one specified sector of the economy. Thus, there are mutual funds that invest exclusively in sectors such as software, fast moving consumer goods (FMCG), pharmaceuticals, petroleum, etc. The returns from these funds are directly linked to the performance of the respective sectors, or industries in which the fund is invested. While these funds may, no doubt, give higher returns if the sector or industry concerned happens to be the flavour of the season, but this positive point is often counterbalanced by the high risks that they carry compared to diversified funds.

Tax saving funds

These funds offer tax rebates (20 per cent for incomes below Rs. 1.5 lakh and 15 per cent for incomes below Rs. 5 lakh) u/s 88 of the Income Tax Act, 1961 on investments up to an annual limit of Rs. 10,000 per individual. These funds, like equity and sector funds, aim for high growth since they have access to funds which have a lock-in period of a minimum of three years. This holding period of three years enables their fund managers to take a comparatively longer view of the markets. It also by and large enables them to report a better performance than equity and sector funds.

Balanced funds

Balanced funds provide both capital appreciation and income. They do so by investing in a "balanced" portfolio composed of stocks, bonds, and money market instruments, in other words in both equity and fixed income securities. The weightage given to equities and to fixed income securities in the composition of the fund is as laid out in fund's offer document.

In a bull market balanced funds do not perform as well as equity and equity-oriented funds, whereas in a bear market they do not fall as much, or as fast, as equity funds do. On the other hand, in a bull market they outperform income funds, but give a relatively poor performance compared to income funds in a bear market. These funds provide an ideal investment vehicle for conservative investors since they are less volatile and less risky than equity funds, but give higher returns than income funds.

Monthly Income Plans (MIPs) are a type of balanced fund where the equity portion is restricted to around 15-20 per cent of the total corpus of the fund. The objective of these funds is to provide a reasonable monthly income through dividends along with some capital appreciation.

Advantages

Investing in mutual funds has three major advantages:

(1) When you invest in a mutual fund you are entrusting your money to full-time professional money-managers who make all the investment decisions on your behalf. This is a major advantage for small investors who lack sufficient knowledge and experience to launch out on their own and also cannot afford, or do not have access to, high-calibre and expensive investment advisors or services. Also, mutual funds are a convenient investment option for investors who do not have the temperament or the time for the exacting homework required to watch over and manage their portfolio of shares. Successful stock market investing requires knowledge, time, a cool head and emotional detachment — qualities which professional mutual fund managers are likely to possess.

(2) Mutual funds enable you to get the full benefit of diversification which you may not be able to achieve when you are investing small sums of money on your own. The minimum amount required to build a reasonably diversified portfolio would be around Rs 5 lakh. A mutual fund, on the other hand, enables you to get the benefits of a diversified portfolio with an investment, as low as Rs. 5,000 to Rs. 10,000. If you manage your own investments then it may take you as long as six months, or even one year, to build a large and well-diversified portfolio. By

investing in a mutual fund, on the other hand, you get the benefit of instant diversification by buying units of even one equity fund.

(3) By virtue of their large asset base and shareholder population, unit of mutual funds enjoy greater liquidity than most company shares. Open-end funds are generally more liquid than closed-end funds. If you have investible funds which you may require at short notice, then mutual funds often offer a better and more convenient investment choice.

Disadvantages

There are basically two disadvantages of investing in mutual funds:

(1) Professional money-managers who manage mutual funds tend to be conservative, risk-aversive and unimaginative. As a result, they generally cannot take bold, timely decisions which are quite often required for earning really big profits. Also, since they are usually under considerable pressure to produce short-term results they are less inclined to take a long-term view and thus miss out on the really big long-term gains.

(2) Mutual funds provide the advantages of diversification but deny you the advantage of concentration. In certain special situations in the stock market, an investment strategy based on concentration can give you vastly superior returns than one based on diversification. Investment and trading strategies based on concentration, however, are strictly for professionals and knowledgeable investors. For beginners and inexperienced investors, we advise diversification for greater safety of returns.

Net asset value (NAV)

When you invest in mutual funds the most important financial indicator (or ratio) that you need to know and understand is Net Asset Value (NAV). The NAV of a fund is equal to its total assets, i.e., market value of shares plus cash balances, minus operational and other expenses divided by the total number of units issued by the fund:

$$\text{Net Asset Value (NAV)} = \frac{\text{(Market value of shares + Cash balances) less Operational expenses}}{\text{Total number of units}}$$

NAV is a very useful ratio. It tells you what each individual unit issued by the fund is worth at any given point of time. For example, if the NAV of a fund is Rs. 22.35 per unit on any given date it means that if the fund were to be liquidated on that date, each share of the fund would fetch you a sum of Rs 22.35.

The NAV also helps you to evaluate and keep track of a fund's performance and for comparing the performance of different funds.

Investor complaints and grievances

SEBI seeks to ensure that only persons of integrity and reputation for fair dealings become trustees who, in turn, keep an eye on who is appointed a director in an asset management company. Various qualifications and disqualifications have been provided in the regulations to keep out people of disrepute.

If a unit holder is aggrieved by the actions of the AMC, and the grievance is not satisfactorily redressed by the investor relations officer, then the doors of SEBI would be a good place to knock. SEBI forwards the complaints to the AMC. This puts an additional pressure on the AMC to redress the grievance.

Investor Relations Officer

Every AMC has an investor relations officer whom unit holders can approach for redressal of grievances. The track record of the AMC in redressing investor complaints, including specifics of number of complaints and the time period when they were redressed needs to be disclosed in the Offer Document. This ensures that AMCs take an interest in sorting out investor complaints.

CHAPTER 13

Tips for successful investing

There is no assured route for achieving investment success, nor for that matter is there any cut-and-dried, instantly- applicable, sure-shot formula for making money in the stock market. There are no high-flying stock market geniuses or financial wizards either. Leaving aside the lucky few who make pots of money within a short span of time, for most other people investing in the stock market is just like any other business. It takes time, patience, hard work and perseverance to achieve success. However, there is one redeeming feature about stock market investments that singles them out for favourable attention. Over the next ten to twenty years, the Indian capital and stock markets are going to offer some of the best and most lucrative opportunities to make big money compared to most other investment avenues. This collection of tips has been given with a view to help you take advantage of these opportunities.

Many of these tips may appear contradictory and confusing. Don't let that perplex you. All roads to investment success are equally valid and all of them have strong points in their favour and disfavour. The stock market is a place where every theory, even the most unlikely one, has its day and where even the most outlandish theories have, at some time or another, achieved spectacular success. The only drawback is that most theories do not work with all people. Each speculator and/or investor has to select and formulate his own theory, plan or method, based on his own temperament, capabilities, objectives and the given situation in which he finds himself. The tips given in this chapter have been selected keeping in mind the requirements, needs and capabilities of a broad spectrum of individual investors and the kind of investment environment in which they are likely to operate over the coming ten years.

Basic principles

Do not invest in unlisted shares

This is the first basic principle for profitable stock market investment.

Invest in active shares

Invest only in shares that are traded frequently on the stock exchange, preferably at least 3-4 times a week. Give preference to shares that are traded regularly on more than one stock exchange.

Diversify your investments

Do not put all your money into shares of any one company or industry — spread it over ten or twenty companies. Diversification minimises risks, lends stability to your portfolio and ensures safety of capital.

Don't over-diversify

Excessive diversification, for example, portfolio of shares of 80 to 90 companies, puts a limit on high returns without commensurate compensation in the form of added safety. Over-diversification is nothing more or less than average investing for average returns. Shares in, say, ten companies engaged in eight to ten different industries generally provide sufficient diversification.

Ensure liquidity of your investment

A liquid investment is one which can be easily sold. Buy only liquid shares, not shares which you may later have difficulty in selling. In other words, do not block your money by purchasing shares for which you may not be able to find ready buyers when you want to sell them.

In all investments there is a trade-off between reward and risk

High-return investments usually carry high risks, whereas low-return investments carry lower risks. Try to strike a balance between reward and risk while making your investment selections.

Investment risks can be reduced through knowledge and experience.

Calculated investment decisions carry lower risks than blind, impulsive decisions taken without adequate information and analysis. Experience and knowledge minimise exposure to investment risk. Therefore, keep yourself well informed, do your investment homework and get competent and informed investment advice before you take a buy or sell decision.

Understanding the stock markets

The stock markets always over-react

They over-react both when they rise and when they fall. This is a basic truth applicable to stock markets all over the world. Over-reaction is what gives rise to booms and depressions. In a bull or rising market, share prices shoot past their intrinsic values to reach dizzy heights; whereas in a bear or falling market, they plummet to depths far below their intrinsic worth. These over-reactions provide opportunities to intelligent investors for making money.

Stock market prices never go straight up or straight down

They always move in short up and down spurts, i.e. in a zigzag pattern. Every rise is followed by a fall, called a reaction — and every fall is followed by a rise which is called a rally. You should make use of this universally observed stock market behaviour for timing your buy and sell decisions.

Greed and fear are the two most dominant emotions that influence stock market behaviour

Greed is the dominant, all-pervasive emotion that fuels a boom, whereas fear eclipses all other emotions in a falling market. Greed and fear are what lead to stock market over-reactions.

The stock markets are irrational in the short-run, but rational over the long-term

Day-to-day, week-to-week share price movements are governed by rumours, gossip, tips, misinformation, crowd behaviour, mass psychology and knee-jerk reactions to news headlines and breaking news. This is the main reason why it is so difficult to understand, interpret and predict short-term share price movements. In the long-term (generally over one year) on the other hand, the price of a share tends to converge towards its intrinsic value. In other words, over the long term violent price fluctuations tend to get flattened out, thus enabling price and value to match. This is also the main reason why it is generally easier to understand and forecast long-term price trends with greater accuracy. Therefore, it is always advisable to bank on the underlying long-term trends while making your investment decisions, and not focus on erratic short-term price fluctuations.

Tactics and strategy

Do not speculate unless you have a natural flair for it

Speculators do not always make more money than investors. On the other hand, they have been seen to lose more money, and in a far shorter period of time, than most investors. Speculation includes buying and selling of shares on margins, buying and selling with a view to making money from short-term fluctuations in share prices, and from short selling. Speculation is a high-risk business where the percentage of failure is very high and the potential rewards are not all that attractive to justify the risks taken.

When investing in shares go for the long-term investments

The long-term equity investor, who has a time horizon of three years or more, is on far safer ground than is the speculator. The former very rarely loses money and his investment returns are generally more certain and assured than those of the speculator. The long-term investor is also in a position to take advantage of the various tax rebates and concessions available on long-term capital gains. On the whole, most long-term investors generally end up making far more money than do most speculators.

The stock markets are dominated by short-term traders and speculators

Stockbrokers are, typically, commission-oriented, and tend to favour short-term traders and investors for obvious reasons. Investment advisors and counsellors also generally favour short-term investments because they function under constant pressure from clients to produce quick results. As a result, long-term investors face very little competition, and this explains why magnificent long-term investment opportunities often go abegging in the stock market. This is another reason in favour of long-term investments.

If you must buy and sell frequently, use the major cyclical swings in the market

Watch the stock market indices to find out when such swings are likely to occur. Buy when the market is close to its cyclical bottom, and sell when the market is close to its top. Buying and selling in line with the major cyclical swings is an easy-to-use and fairly successful stock market trading strategy. It also carries lower risks than short-term trading and speculation.

Vertically integrated, single-product companies offer better investment opportunities than diversified companies

A vertically integrated company is one which has integrated its operations from the raw material stage to the finished product. Reliance Industries and Tisco (Tata Iron & Steel Co) are examples of such companies.

Companies that manufacture and/or market consumer products are generally steadier and sounder investments

Shares of such companies are less prone to volatile price fluctuations than of those that operate in the core sectors of the economy. This again is a broad generalisation that admits of many exceptions.

Bank on growth, growth, growth

When selecting shares to buy, try to stack the odds in your favour. A good, time-tested way of doing this would be to buy shares in a growth company, managed or controlled by a growing business house, belonging to a growing industry, and operating in a growing sector of the economy.

Invest in companies with a low price earnings ratios (P/E)

Companies with low P/E ratios often offer better investment value than those which have a high P/E. When you invest in a company with a low P/E, you give yourself two chances to win whereas with a company with a high P/E you have only one chance. In the former case, you gain not only from an improvement in the company's profits and earnings per share but also from an upward re-rating of its P/E ratio. In the latter case, the opportunity to gain from an upward movement of the P/E ratio is limited, if not completely non-existent.

The best investment opportunities always exist in the most unlikely places

This is an invaluable, rule-of-thumb technique for picking potential stock market winners. Therefore, develop the habit of looking closely at "neglected" and "overlooked" companies operating in the less visible sectors of the economy for high-growth investment opportunities.

Buy shares in companies that are currently out of favour

Out-of-favour companies, particularly blue chip companies that are temporarily going through a spell of bad luck, can be great investment opportunities. Since these shares are out of favour, their prices cannot fall any further because they have already touched rock-bottom levels.

Don't confuse a share's intrinsic worth with its market price

A share is high-priced or low-priced in relation to its intrinsic value and not on the strength of its ruling share price.

"Buy dear, sell dearer" is generally a better investment strategy than "buy cheap and sell dear"

Quite often cheap shares tend to remain cheap and apparent bargains sink further whereas apparently expensive shares tend to rise even higher over time.

Never hold on to a share which you wouldn't buy at its current price

The reasons for holding on to a share are the same as those for buying it. If you are not prepared to buy a particular share at its ruling market price, then there is no reason why you should hold on to it either. A share is either worth buying or worth selling, there is no such thing as holding on to a share. The mere fact that you own or possess a particular share should not be allowed to alter or cloud your basic perception of what the share is worth. The decision to "hold" is basically a "buy" decision masquerading in a different garb and under a different name. Try to view and treat all "hold" decisions as different versions of a "buy" decision, for clearer investment thinking. (The decision to hold acquires a special significance of its own only when extraneous considerations like tax payments, set-off of capital losses against capital gains, etc. enter into the decision-making process).

Beware of bargain hunting in the stock markets

There is a lot of competition in this field. All investors, speculators, stockbrokers, investment analysts and investment advisors are engaged in it all the time. It is the most popular and widely played game in the market. The chances of your discovering and picking up a genuine bargain or super-bargain before somebody else does are quite remote. Whenever you spot a share that looks like a bargain, give it a closer look and subject it to detailed scrutiny and analysis, because there is bound to be a snag in it somewhere. Most shares which appear to be bargains generally turn out to be discarded shares with poor saleability and dismal future prospects. Therefore, leave bargain hunting to investment professionals and specialists.

Don't put too much reliance on charts and technical analysis

Charts and graphs do not foretell the future — they only give a picture of the past. Moreover, they function best in free and uncontrolled markets where the forces of demand and supply can interact with each other in an unrestricted manner. In the Indian stock markets where there are few effective checks on insider trading, where margin rates are changed frequently to moderate bull and bear pressures, and where financial institutions sometimes push up or force down prices on government dictated considerations, suitable conditions for the free interplay of market forces do not fully exist.

Be on the lookout for rights renunciations

A large number of shareholders sell their entitlement to rights shares in the stock market. These rights renunciations are generally available at a price far lower than the ruling market price for that particular company's shares. Take advantage of this by buying rights renunciations of good companies.

Selecting which share to buy is always easier than when to buy it

Selection depends on quantifiable, and calculable criteria, whereas timing depends upon judgement, intuition, understanding of mass psychology and an ability to outguess the market. Therefore, always try to undo and offset the possible adverse effects of bad timing through superior investment selection.

It is harder to take good selling decisions than good buying decisions

This is because too many emotional and other extraneous considerations tend to enter into a selling decision, which is not the case in a buying decision. This is another reason why long-term investment strategies generally give superior results than short-term, in-and-out trading strategies.

Averaging up is a sound investment strategy

It works something like this: Once you decide to buy a share don't buy all the number you want at one time. Buy a small number first and closely watch the share's price movements. An upward movement of the share price will help to confirm that your earlier judgement was right. Then you buy more shares and expand your shareholding. This process is repeated. You buy more and more shares with each upward movement in the share price. This investment strategy is called averaging up or pyramiding.

Never average down

It is a poor investment strategy. Most people resort to averaging down in the hope of bringing down their average purchase costs. This is undeniably true, but if share prices continue to slide downwards and do not make the quick U-turn that you expect then you actually end up multiplying your losses. A better investment strategy would be to wait for the downtrend to reach the bottom of the "U" before you resume buying. Always buy on the upswing and never on the downswing.

Don't invest in new issues of new companies promoted by unknown and untried managements

Such companies have a high percentage of failure.

A company is generally as good or as bad as its management

You will never find a good company with a bad management or a bad company with a good management. The quality of a company's management is often more important than its quantifiable financial indicators. If you bank on good management, you can never really go wrong with your investment selections. As a corollary to this rule, avoid investing in companies that have a history or a background of factionalism and management infighting.

Invest in companies which have a clearly identifiable plus factor

A distinct advantage gives a company leadership in its chosen field and makes all the difference between success and failure. This plus factor can be either superior technological skills, superior corporate planning, superior marketing techniques combined with a bigger and more effective marketing network, superior products or superior financial and tax planning.

APPENDIX A

Sources of information

Newspapers

Hindu Business Line
The Economic Times
The Financial Express
The Business Standard

Magazines

Capital Market
Business India
Business World
Business Today
Outlook Money
Dalal Street Journal
Bajaj Capital Investors India

Websites

www.bseindia.com
www.nseindia.com
www.sebi.gov.in
www.equitymaster.com
www.sharekhan.com
www.capitalmarket.com
www.indiabulls.com
www.moneycontrol.com
www.mutualfundsindia.com
www.myiris.com
www.nsdl.co.in
www.icicidirect.com
www.indiainfoline.com
www.investsmartindia.com
www.capitalideasonline.com

Important addresses

BSE Head Office

The Stock Exchange,
Phiroze Jeejeebhoy Towers,
Dalal Street, Mumbai - 400001
Tel: 91-22-22721233/4
Fax: 91-22-22721552
Web:www.bseindia.com

NSE Corporate Office

National Stock Exchange of India Ltd.
Exchange Plaza,
Plot no. C/1, G Block,
Bandra-Kurla Complex
Bandra (E)
Mumbai - 400051.
Tel No: (022) 26598100 - 8114
Web: www.nseindia.com

SEBI Head Office

Securities and Exchange Board of India
Mittal Court, "B" Wing, 1st Floor,
224, Nariman Point,
Mumbai: 400021.
Tel:+91-22-22850451-56, 22880962-70.
Fax:+91-22 22045633 / 22021073.
Web: www.sebi.gov.in

APPENDIX B

Composition of stock indices

NIFTY (50)

Reliance Industries
Hindustan Lever
Wipro
Infosys Technologies
State Bank of India
ITC
GAIL
SAIL
Ranbaxy Laboratories
ICICI Bank
Tata Motors
TISCO
HDFC
Hindustan Petroleum
BPCL
BHEL
Larsen & Turbo
Hindalco
Dr. Reddy's Lab.
National Alu
Satyam Computer
HDFC Bank
Grasim Inds.
Bajaj Auto
HCL Technologies
Hero Honda
MTNL
BSES
Tata Power
Cipla
Zee Telefilms
Sun Pharma
Oriental Bank
IPCL
Shipping Corporation
M & M
VSNL
Gujarat Ambuja Cement
ACC
Glaxosmith. Phr
ABB
Dabur
Digital Global
Tata Chemicals
Colgate
Indian Hotel
Tata Tea
Britannia
Glaxosmith.Con
NIIT

BSE SENSEX (30)

Reliance Industries
Infosys Technologies
Hindustan Lever
ICICI Bank
ITC
State Bank of India
Ranbaxy Laboratories
Larsen & Turbo
Tata Steel
HDFC
Tata Motors
Hindalco Inds.
Satyam Computer
HDFC Bank
Grasim Inds.
Dr. Reddy's Lab.
Wipro
Hindustan Petroleum
Bajaj Auto
ONGC
Tata Power
Bharti Tele Venture
BHEL
Cipla
Hero Honda Motors
ACC
MTNL
BSES
Gujarat Ambuja Cement
Zee Telefilms

APPENDIX C

Compound interest table

This table shows the compound rate of growth of Re. 1 with the interest being compounded yearly.

Interest	*Number of Years*								
Rate	*2*	*3*	*4*	*5*	*6*	*7*	*8*	*9*	*10*
10%	1.21	1.33	1.46	1.61	1.77	1.95	2.14	2.36	2.59
11%	1.23	1.37	1.52	1.69	1.87	2.08	2.31	2.56	2.84
12%	1.25	1.41	1.57	1.76	1.97	2.21	2.48	2.77	3.11
13%	1.28	1.44	1.63	1.84	2.08	2.35	2.66	3.00	3.40
14%	1.30	1.48	1.69	1.93	2.20	2.50	2.85	3.25	3.70
15%	1.32	1.52	1.75	2.01	2.31	2.66	3.06	3.52	4.05
16%	1.35	1.56	1.81	2.10	2.44	2.83	3.28	3.80	4.41
17%	1.37	1.60	1.87	2.19	2.57	3.00	3.51	4.11	4.87
18%	1.39	1.64	1.94	2.29	2.70	3.19	3.76	4.44	5.23
19%	1.42	1.69	2.01	2.39	2.84	3.37	4.02	4.79	5.70
20%	1.44	1.73	2.07	2.49	2.98	3.58	4.30	5.16	6.19
21%	1.46	1.77	2.14	2.59	3.14	3.18	4.60	5.56	6.73
22%	1.49	1.82	2.22	2.70	3.30	4.02	4.91	5.99	7.31
23%	1.51	1.86	2.29	2.81	3.46	4.26	5.24	6.44	7.92
24%	1.54	1.91	2.36	2.93	3.63	4.50	5.59	6.93	8.59
25%	1.56	1.95	2.44	3.05	3.81	4.77	5.96	7.45	9.31
26%	1.59	2.00	2.52	3.17	4.00	5.04	6.35	8.00	10.09
27%	1.61	2.05	2.60	3.30	4.19	5.33	6.77	8.60	10.71
28%	1.64	2.10	2.68	3.44	4.40	5.63	7.21	9.22	11.81
29%	1.66	2.15	2.77	3.57	4.61	5.95	7.67	9.90	12.76
30%	1.69	2.20	2.86	3.71	4.83	6.27	8.16	10.60	12.79
31%	1.72	2.25	2.95	3.86	5.05	6.62	8.67	11.36	14.88
32%	1.74	2.30	3.04	4.01	5.29	6.98	9.22	12.17	16.06
33%	1.77	2.35	3.13	4.16	5.54	7.36	9.79	13.02	17.32
34%	1.80	2.41	3.22	4.32	5.79	7.76	10.40	13.93	18.67
35%	1.82	2.46	3.32	4.48	6.05	8.17	11.03	14.69	20.11
40%	1.96	2.74	3.84	5.39	7.53	10.54	14.76	20.66	28.93
45%	2.10	3.05	4.42	6.41	9.29	13.48	19.54	28.33	41.09
50%	2.25	3.38	5.06	7.59	11.39	17.09	25.63	38.44	57.67

Note:

(a) An investment of Re 1 growing at the compound rate of 15 per cent per annum would become Rs. 2.01 after a period of 5 years. In other words, any investment, which grows at the rate of 15 per cent, will double in 5 years.

(b) An investment of Rs. 5,000 growing at a compound rate of 25 per cent per annum would become Rs. 15,000 (Rs. 5,000 x 3.05) after the same period of 5 years.

(c) Suppose you want to find out at which rate of growth your investment has been growing. If your investment has grown by 10.09 times in 10 years, then by using the table you can find out that you have been growing at the compound rate of growth of 26 per cent per annum.

Index